By the Way of the Border

Travels around the frontiers and beyuls of Nepal

By the **WAY** of the **BORDER**

Travels around the frontiers and beyuls of Nepal

Maximillian Mørch

VAJRA BOOKS

Published and Distributed 2019 by
Vajra Books
Jyatha, Thamel, P.O. Box 21779, Kathmandu, Nepal
Tel.: 977-1-4220562, 4246536
e-mail: vajrabooksktm@gmail.com
www.vajrabooks.com.np

Cover Photo credits: Herman Thapa

ISBN 978-9937-9330-0-1

Printed in Nepal

Contents

Acknowledgments

This book would not have been written were it not for the advice and idea generated in countless discussions with a number of friends, too many to mention, but in particular from Devjit Roy Chowdhury, Nirnaya Bhatta and Quincy Wiele.

My thanks goes to Herman Thapa for his endless support and for being a great and resourceful travelling companion, who also provided some fantastic photos of Rolwaling, including the cover photo.

I would also like to thank Deepak Jha in Saptari for guidance on the Madesh, and I extend my gratitude to all the guides and fixers I met along the way, particularly Suresh Tharu and Narayan Baral. Very little in this book would have happened without them.

The publication of this book would not have been possible without Bidur and Lokesh Dangol from Vajra Books and their help in both designing the book and for placing faith in the project.

Finally, this book is dedicated to my mother and father; for starting me on this journey. My only regret is that it came too late for my father to read.

Introduction

This book was written during my time as a post-graduate student at Tribhuvan University. I have written about the country and its history, which have completely dominated my thoughts for the last three years. This is not a comprehensive analysis of Nepali politics, development or society; there are already many books on those subjects. Nor is this a collection of tales about extreme mountaineering endeavours; there are already many books about that too. This is instead, a collection of tales about journeys I made in remote regions of Nepal, regions that do not appear in the majority of travel literature.

The trip to Far-West Nepal took place in early 2017. This trip was part of my research for my master's thesis and I have omitted many parts relating to my actual research, as they would be of little interest to the reader. The Rolwaling valley trek took place in February 2016, and the trip to eastern Nepal took place during April and May 2017.

I am not a historian, so I have leant heavily on other sources for historical information. I have included a list of these sources at the end of the book. For the sake of privacy, I have changed the names of some of the people I met on my travels.

Kathmandu, 2017

The Far-West
and Api Nampa

Kathmandu to
Bardia National Park

I walked through Thamel, Kathmandu's tourist mecca, looking for a bus ticket. Over the last 30 years, Thamel has gained a permanent place in traveller folklore. Thamel has it all, from hotels, restaurants, laundry services and bars to gaudy shops and signs that loudly proclaim a selection of - often misspelled – food items such as 'Non-veg tit bits' and 'Chewmin'. Thamel is where the overwhelming majority of travel agencies are based, allowing easy access to a multitude of rafting and trekking trips. As a result, ultra-serious European trekkers walk the same streets as elderly tour groups and nouveau hippies with the latest iPhones; they all congeal in Thamel. Yet, while Thamel remains all smiles, and is for most merely a setting for drinks, souvenirs and dodgy food, beneath the hash and parties you can glimpse Thamel's dark underbelly of prostitution, addiction and sporadic gang violence.

Picking my way past taxis and tourists and avoiding the glances of hash sellers on the street, I walked into one of the many ubiquitous travel agencies that line Thamel's crowded streets. I booked a bus trip to Bardia National Park, a gruelling fifteen-hour, overnight ride from Kathmandu. Bardia is well known for its abundance of wildlife, as well as reportedly being the best place to spot the illusive Bengal tiger and the increasingly rare Gangetic dolphin. More importantly – for me, at least – Bardia was over 500 km west of Kathmandu and was as convenient a stop on my way to Darchula as I could think of. I had long read about Bardia, yet due to work and other commitments, I had never had time to make the trip. Now I did.

I arrived at Gongabu Bus Park at 2 p.m., and after a departure miraculously close to the scheduled departure time, the bus pulled out of the station and set off on a slow and lumbering journey to the south eastern plains of Nepal. The bus laboured through the Kathmandu traffic, tortuously making its way to Kalanki and the road out of Kathmandu. Almost two hours after setting out and already dusty, we snaked our way past Naubise and onto the Prithvi Highway. The road followed the Trisuli River, and soon we had left the city far behind, travelling at relatively breakneck speed – for our bus, at least – on our way to Mugling and the turnoff to the Terai, the southern plains that stretched out across the country's border with India. Rattling along the highway, I saw that our bus, the aptly named Bardia Bullet, was rather empty, although the conductor was trying to rectify the situation by getting as many roadside stragglers onto the bus as possible. Turning off at Mugling, we headed down to Narayanghat. This section of road was always under improvement, and yet, it mysteriously never improved. Almost two hours later, we finally arrived – battered but not bruised – in the Terai.

The Terai makes up the majority of Nepal's landmass and population. Life was different on the plains compared to up in the hills—that was certain.

As the bus turned east and we picked up speed on the mercifully flat roads of the Terai, the sun started to set over the rice fields. In the crimson light, I saw no sign of the KichKandi, the beautiful, mythical women who wander the highway in white saris, luring lonesome travellers astray. They are often formed when, after an untimely death, a woman is not fully cremated, leaving her spirit to roam. Their backwards feet indicate that they are tormented spirits, forced to wander the sites of their deaths.

Through the night, the bus trundled along without incident, save the odd horn and close encounter with a bullock cart. I closed my eyes, rocked by the steady movements of the bus, and pretended to sleep.

It was past eight the next morning when the bus arrived. Bleary-eyed and weary, I got off the bus at Tharukwada and was met by Suresh, my guide for the trip. I was glad to be off the bus and able to stretch my legs. Suresh took me to my hotel in a small Jeep.

The hotel had been recommend by a friend of mine, yet walking around it was impossible to shake the feeling that no one was there. That was because no one was. I had, as it turned out, the hotel to myself for the next few days, which was both equally good and bad news. I peered in to the hotel's bar, the one thing more depressing than drinking in a sad dusty old bar, was drinking in a sad dusty old bar with there being no-one else there to complain about it to.

After dropping my bags off at the hotel we drove down on Suresh's bike to Rajapur, at the mouth of the Karnali River to look for river dolphins. I had first heard of the existence of Gangetic dolphins in Nepal from a friend, while he himself had never seen them his guide had stressed there were still many left. This, I had to see. Nepal is host to several tributaries of the Ganges, and several of these rivers supposedly contain river dolphins, although reports of their numbers were rather erratic.

The Karnali River is famous for its size, being the longest in Nepal and serves as the division between Bardia and Kailali districts. The riverhead of the Karnali starts in the Mapchachuo glacier as a mere trickle, before assuming its eventual wide flow through western Nepal. It has also recently become more famous for one of the biggest and most iconic bridges in Nepal at Chisopani, built by the Japanese. While it was indeed big I decided to disbelieve Suresh, and anyone else in fact, however earnestly when they tried to convince me the Chisopani Bridge was in fact a tourist attraction, let alone world famous.

We headed back down the East-West Highway on Suresh's Honda heading for Rajapur, in Bardia district. Turning off the main road we rode for almost half an hour down a road that became increasingly dusty and bumpy as it went on until the road seemingly stopped altogether. It was now just a trail of sand flanked by bushes and we were now almost half a foot deep in sand. Yet nevertheless half an hour later we pulled up at the banks of the Karnali, just north of the Indian border.

Here the Karnali is fragmented and disjointed, flowing erratically through a wide river basin. Straight away I heard and noticed a large number of birds, while Suresh immediately concerned himself with looking for the ripple of the dolphins as they come up to breathe. I had seen dolphins many times before, but always in the sea and whilst on a boat. The last time I'd seen them was in a blustery North Sea in March while crossing from Belfast to Stranraer. This was slightly different. There was something alluring about being able to sit on the bank of a river, hundreds of kilometres inland and watch dolphins. After all the Bay of Bengal was far away. We sat down to wait. With huge environmental and social changes in the Gangetic Basin, including the construction of hydropower projects, their habitat is increasingly under threat. Like with many other species of wildlife living in Nepal, there is a real race against time to see these animals in the wild.

After sitting idly by and waiting for an hour for dolphins to make their appearance we had seen no site of them, I therefore turned my attention back inland. This was as beautiful and an atypical section of the Terai you could find. Lush rice paddies made up the foreground, and in the background distant trees are the highest things around apart from the birds. In the distance farmers walked between and ploughed their fields, many still using a buffalo and wooden plough.

Were it not for the tyre marks on the road behind me or the odd power cable, this is a scene that has remained almost unchanged for centuries. The smell of the fields is rich and pungent. With an average height of 100metres above sea level, the Terai is vastly different from the Siwilak hills you can see outlined faintly to the north. Yet the wildlife is the most alluring part of the Terai, with cows grazing, buffalos ploughing fields and bathing in mud, a welcome respite from the forlorn dust covered cattle that battle traffic in Kathmandu. Here we were safely far away enough from the East-West highway to no longer hear and feel the trucks rolling past behind us. Bird calls, for now at least, were noise enough.

Yet the serenity of the Terai's countryside often lies directly at odds with its politics. The Terai people have often been historically overlooked by the Paharias, much more commonly associated with Nepal. With people from the plains having a noticeably darker complexion, different linguistical history and the plains being home to the largest Muslim population in the country, they have long been ignored and cast off simply as 'Indians'. The lack of space for the Madheshi in the Nepali national identity gave way to the Madheshi Anadalon in 2007, and has continued to cause protests and disturb what little semblance of stability Nepal wearily clings onto. The politics of the Madhesh were nefarious, notoriously fiendish and difficult, and to an outsider seemed overwhelmingly almost set up to impede and hinder any form of progress or consensus whatsoever.

Disturbing me from my thoughts with a whispered hiss, Suresh grabbed my arm and pointed downstream. '*I think I saw a dolphin come up for air*'. We headed down stream to get a better look. I knew we could not be far from the Indian border, yet I had no idea just how close we in fact were. The border is marked by white pillars, yet some have been damaged or simply fallen apart from heavy weathering. As a result it was after we had walked for about 30 seconds that we came to a small dirt path, heading horizontal to the river, and behind we saw the same river, paddies and farming land we saw before. No change there then. Except that due to the existence of a small off-white pillar parallel with the path we were stood upon the border between Nepal and India. We sat down on the riverbank by the border and continued to try to pick up the trail of bubbles breaking on the surface.

After only several minutes wait we were rewarded with the burst of a dorsal fin followed by a small grey Gangetic dolphin breaking the surface of the water. Staying where we where we could observe its movements and follow it darting up and back downstream. Every two to three minutes it would resurface, roughly in the same area, for all of half a second. After watching the dolphin unknowingly cross the border back and forth, we left it behind and headed back toward the motorbike. We were close to Tikapur which had become infamous for events in 2016 during the political crisis. While the Terai became a political tinderbox, events in Tikapur had gained notoriety around the country. Following continued riots, protests and deaths, seven policemen were killed and one of the policemen was burned alive by protestors. Tragically the two-year-old son of the APF senior head constable also died during the protests.

I could still vividly remember that day, when at university in Kathmandu alongside a number of Nepal security force officers and a general, we first heard the news. With reports the army could be deployed, you could have cut the tension with a knife.

Yet now in Tikapur, while tensions had now settled, if they were to flare up again it could well be here. However holding heated political discussions was not why I came to Tikapur. I had heard about the Royal Gardens in Tikapur and being in the area I wanted to check them out. Previously having been owned by the Royal Family, they were supposed to be a lush oasis in relative isolation. First built by King Mahendra as a private garden, who built a small wooden cottage in the middle, his son King Dipendra had then also built a house in the same park. Since 2008 following the overthrow of the monarchy, it was now open to the public. These old royal parks and spaces fascinated me, as did the royal palace in Kathmandu. Like many old public gardens or houses you could see the vestiges of former glory, but these days you had to look harder and in places you really had to want to see what you thought you did.

The entrance was deserted and dilapidated, we parked the bike next to the only other one around and headed inside. We walked past the closed ticket counter, only to get called back. We had thought the counter was closed, but the man had simply been laying back on his chair out of site with the blind over his window. After paying the nominal entrance fee, we entered the park.

The Royal Gardens of Tikapur were established by King Mahendra as the quiet natural environment was thought to have a beneficial effect upon the king's health. I wondered as we walked through the park what Mahendra would have thought about when he too, strolled through the park. We walked through a large set of grounds, with all sides being marked by large trees and bushes. Yet most of the shrubbery lay dying and some plantation areas were barren.

Mahendra's house, or Mahendra Arogya Griha, was a small wooden cottage, with brown panelling and a thatched roof. Alas, it was completely empty, with mere dust for contents.

Former king Dipendra's house, a little more garish and in slightly strange design. Again I hopped up to the windows. While it was again almost empty and full with dust, I could make out a large, but ultimately empty drinks cabinet. The traces of the monarchy's existence in this park now consisted of two empty buildings and a park now filled with couples tentatively holding hands.

There was now little to show this was once the private palatial gardens of Nepal's monarchs. I tried to imagine armed security patrolling the area, lush oasis of plants and trees, a helicopter waiting to ferry members of the Royal family and most of all I tried to imagine Mahendra or Dipendra walking around the same garden I was. Yet I couldn't. The damaged and frayed fence, patchy grass and general shabbiness mean it was long removed from the luxurious oasis I had imagined back in Kathmandu.

We walked through the park, talking politics and I cautiously asked Suresh on his own politics. He didn't want to talk about it. We walked over a trampled fence and came again to the banks of the Karnali. Outside the park, it appears security measures have lapsed a little since the park was placed into public ownership. Having seen enough and wanting to be back before dark we left. As I rode back along the border to the National Park Suresh shouts into my ear a story about a bus and a tiger. Struggling to hear over the wind noise, I make out that just two weeks ago, on this very road, a bus hit and killed a male tiger. The tiger was killed on the spot, but the bus didn't get away unscathed. Having a rough idea of what would happen if two men and a bike came into contact with a tiger, I sped up anxiously trying to get back to the hotel.

That evening, sat alone on a long group dining table I had a chicken cutlet, which was somehow fried yet curried and had the benefit of neither cooking method. I sat and drank a warm beer. There was no-one else in the resort, and most of the staff had gone home, it was again deserted apart from the sounds of the jungle at night. Starved of conversation and not wanting to keep the waiter there any longer than he has to be, I grabbed another warm beer and headed to bed.

For the first day in the Park, I had arranged for a jeep safari. The next morning sitting, again alone at the end of my overtly large dining table I started to eat breakfast. Although the breakfast was of the same quality of last night, it took marginally longer to eat, on account of me attempting to fish all the ants out of the jam before spreading it on my untoasted toast. I had to soon give up on this endeavour, there were simply too many. Somehow one portion of the bread was burnt and all the rest wasn't touched. It looked as if it had been toasted using a lighter. Having swallowed down a proportion of my breakfast I headed out and waited until the jeep pulled up.

There was a women in the front of the jeep, that I thought I recognised but wasn't quite sure. Nevertheless I got in the jeep and we set off. After a few minutes or so of her looking back and me, and me looking back at her, she asked whether we knew each other.

It turns out that I already knew her, and had even spent an evening drinking with her. I remember Ashmita being nice company if a little loud. We were also joined by an American, who'd lived in Bardia for several years, he said volunteering but never said what or where. After he said he hadn't spent a lot of time in the park yet spent 10 months a year in Bardia and 2 in the United States fundraising I was suspicious. Finding out he was from the Midwest, I immediately pegged him a missionary which turned out later to be true.

Bardia was established as a National Park in 1988. Its boundaries stretch from the eastern bank of the Karnali, where Suresh and I searched for dolphins to the Babi River and to the Siwalik hills in the north that make up its northern border. The park is on land that was lost in the Sugauli treaty in 1816 and returned in 1860 following Nepal's support for Britain during the 1857 mutiny in India. Like most other national parks it was originally demarcated as a Royal Hunting Reserve in 1969, in 1982 the Royal Bardia Wildlife Reserve, and following expansion to the Babi Valley in 1982, it was finally declared a national park in 1988. As with other national parks, the inhabitants were forced to relocate and resettle outside of the park's boundaries. This had created significant local unrest at the time, however now it does mean the area is perfect for wildlife, and its large size patrolled by the Army has kept poaching under control, which had unfortunately risen to worrying levels during the insurgency.

The park mainly consists of forest, primarily sal trees, and savanna land. Elephants, Rhinos and Crocodiles have made Bardia their home along with the famed Bengal Tiger. Being significantly further from Kathmandu compared to Chitwan has led to a considerably

Photo 1: The grasslands of Bardia

lower number of tourists arriving at Bardia. Resultantly there has been much less environmental damage from tourists.

We spent most of the day in the jeep, driving from looking tower to riverbanks and back again. Yet apart from a few deer and a distant view of the backside of a Rhino, we didn't see a lot. Although whether the primary reason for that was the continuous diesel rattle of the jeep, or by Asmita increasingly loud plea's to the Tigers to emerge I will never know. In the evening we waited for a good, or bad depending on how you look at it, a few hours waiting by a riverbank for a tiger, yet nothing came.

On the drive back that night, we dropped off both Asmita and the American at their resorts and drove back to our resort, which was still empty.

Bardia and its surrounding areas are also makeup part of the land of the Tharus, who have long made the Terai their home. The Tharus have an interesting history and are considered indigenous to the area. Their original origin is hard to truly identify, some claim Rajput origin, others claim Sakya and Koilya heritage, others claim they migrated from the Thar Desert in Rajasthan. They claim to be the people of the forest, and existing in relative isolation their livelihoods were dependent upon it. As a result, they enjoy a traditional immunity to Malaria, which also contributed to their isolation, existing in the malarial Terai where seemingly no others could safely dwell. This unique advantage was lost following a USAID/WHO malarial eradication programme using DDT which started in 1954 and preceded a mass influx non-Tharus into what was traditional Tharu land. More land was lost with the formation of both Bardia and Chitwan National Parks. The Tharus have their own language and dialects, and also suffer from a lack of political identity and have no substantial representation. Now many are scattered around the Nepalese Terai, Uttarakhand, Uttar Pradesh and Bihar. Yet while they are recognised as an official nationality in Nepal, there exists a number of subdivisions of Tharus.

Following dinner, I sat in the dining hall. Alone on one of 3 tables meant for 20, I dipped back into my book and drank a now familiarly warm beer before heading to bed. It was slightly surreal being in a resort by my own I felt, the general shabbiness of the resort only added to this feeling.

While jeep drives are a good way of covering ground, they are noisy and after a whole day of warning off animals with the engine noise tend to get rather dull. Going on foot was a different matter.

The next day, loaded up with tiffin's and water, following Suresh we set off early for a full day walking in the jungle. Yesterday had mainly been spent talking and taking in the view, today with just me and Suresh on foot I was much more engaged and involved in animal spotting, or rather reacting to Suresh spotting animals.

It was about 8 am by the time we entered the park and Suresh received a phone call. *'Where are you?* 'his friend asked? *'We've just seen a tiger by the riverbank'.*

Seemingly if we had been in the park just 30 minutes earlier we could have bagged the tiger straight away and would have had the whole day left to wander contentedly. Yet the tiger had come, but it had already drunk its share for the morning, now with its thirst satiated it meant there was potentially less chance of it coming out again soon. Still, it was proof that they did indeed exist and could be seen.

We headed first to a different riverbed, the sand is good for leaving prints and tracking. While one tiger had just been spotted drinking, we were several kilometres away and looking for a different tiger. It wasn't long before we, or rather Suresh, had made a discovery. Fresh prints, with the sand still damp. Not just that but there were two sets of prints, the other belonging to a tiger cub. This was accompanied by several spots of dried blood. As water on sand dried quickly, we knew these were recent and therefore the tiger was nearby. Or in fact, Suresh knew, and he told me. *'Ah this a good sign. The mother and baby must have come here just before to drink. Normally the mother only needs to drink twice a day, the baby needs more. Therefore if we climb a tree and wait, they could come back'.* I nodded. So we did. We both climbed a tree and waited. And continued to wait. Which can be rather difficult in a tree as the branches and knots have a tendency to feel as if they move with your body, forcing you to constantly be uncomfortable, and constantly shift. As we sat in the tree, the morning sun rose to become the baking midday sun. Sitting in the tree starting to drip with sweat, I cursed myself for leaving my bag with water, sun cream, and hat in my bag at the twenty feet below at the bottom of the tree. I could see the river basin in front of me, with tall elephant grass behind me swaying in the wind. If there was anything in the grass behind me, I doubted whether I would be able to differentiate the movement of an animal between the motions of grass blowing in the wind. As a result, I turned my attention to the dusty, but empty, river bank.

The hours passed slowly and soon became a monotonous blur. Occasionally a barking deer would make an appearance but otherwise, we were left alone. We waited for what seemed like the passing of an epoch and still, nothing came. Finally, we gave up and headed into the elephant grass behind us. Visibility was low and there was no path to follow but we kept on walking. It was a good 20 minutes after having left the riverbank that Suresh grabbed my arm urgently, and gestured for me to look for trees to climb. It turns out we had stumbled on a Rhino all of 15 metres ahead, staring right at us. Attempting to walk around it we must have startled it and a few seconds later with a hoot and snort it crashed off through the undergrowth. After that, I would constantly be looking for a suitable tree to climb if the situation came to it. Not that it did.

With a bit more of adrenaline coursing through our veins, we headed faster and deeper through the jungle before arriving at another riverbank. There, we repeated what was fast becoming a ritual, climbing a tree and waiting. Although this time at least, I'd brought my tiffin. We sat in the tree eating rice and curry and waited for something to happen.

Searching for tigers, or any rare and illusive animal is a strange affair. Seeing a tiger isn't make or break for the trip. I'm here to see Bardia, I told myself, and if I see a tiger it would merely be a bonus. After 6 hours of walking around in the heat and waiting in a tree, I began to realise that was a lie. I would be, through no fault of Suresh, annoyed if I didn't see a tiger. Yet I knew how patently irrational that was. All of the waiting and so-called hardships I'd have to go through would be worth it ten times over if I saw one. I think these feelings must be familiar to many.

After lunch, we were still empty-handed, so we went deeper into the jungle. I had seen a rhino, several spotted and barking deer, heard a sloth bear, been constantly surrounded by both Rhesus and Langur Moneys and spent a day walking around a national park. While on safari in many parts of Africa, you're constrained to be being stuck to a jeep and not allowed to walk in a park under any exceptions. Yet here armed with merely a guide and a stick we could roam wherever we wanted. I should have been over the moon but the possibility I might see a tiger had clouded my vision. I doubted the desire was just to see a tiger for myself and not also the possibility of bragging back in Kathmandu of my feline encounter. Wasn't this, I thought, half the problem or paradox, with travel writing. It had predated Facebook and Instagram, in driving people to do things for the stories, as opposed for the sake of doing it, or at least that's what it felt like sometimes.

Later on, we returned to where we had been before the previous day, to sit by a creek and wait. Today, unlike yesterday, there was already a sizeable population camped out. Maybe 20 in all, 10 foreigners and 10 guides. It was a real motley crew, a mixture up of safari hats and expensive camping gear on one side, many of whom had diligently sewn patches of all the national parks and countries they'd been onto the side of their bags, and the usual ragtag collection of travellers on the other side. The guides in their dark green uniforms were no doubt equally amused by both groups. After 10 minutes of waiting there was some commotion to my left. A rhino, possibly this morning's, was nearby and had been spotted by another guide only a couple of hundred metres away. With no sign of the elusive tiger, the animal almost everyone in the groups had openly proclaimed to be here for, the group disbanded almost uniformly in direction of the Rhino.

With no better alternative, I followed slowly behind. It was then after only a few footsteps that yet again Suresh grabbed my arm. *'Max, use your glasses. Look over there'*, and then he pointed to the riverbank, maybe 150 metres away. He'd seen some movement but wasn't able to make out what it was with his naked eye. I placed the binoculars up to my eye and saw the iconic blur of orange and black that makes the tiger so distinctive. It was sitting facing us, lying in the water, seemingly cooling off. It may have been a considerable distance away but its size, strength and sheer power were immediately obvious.

A wave of relief washed over me, I had seen a tiger and immediately became almost embarrassed at how much I was depending, or hoping at least, to see one on this trip. Suresh, after having a good look on the binoculars, went off to tell a guide, his close friend. He wanted his friend's client to get a good view. As Suresh disappeared into the trees behind me, I was left on my own, alone staring at a tiger. Having heard so much about the fabled tiger to see it now was a mixture of excitement, relief and it was accompanied by a sense of validation. Despite having read so many negative forecasts and sorry tales from almost anyone concerned with tigers, there was one right here. It was closer than I could have imagined.

My thoughts were disturbed as I hear a crashing through the bushes, slightly scared for a second, only to groan inwardly as I heard a multitude of voices, in a mixture of English, German and French. *'Tiger, Tiger, Tiger'*, I heard. The next minute the entire group was crowding around where I was standing, jockeying for position. The literal shouts of excitement were surely loud enough for the Tiger to hear, but almost disappointingly it stayed. It would have been a nice bit of schadenfreude had the Tiger been disturbed by their noise and left before they'd all managed to take a photo.

Everyone got their cameras out and for the next few minutes, the air was full of the sound of shutters clicking. Only having a camera phone and being too far away to pick the tiger up on my camera, I

Photo 2: Looking for Tigers

was happy just to look. One American, with a utility belt strapped to his protruding chest with 3 cameras dangling of that, fiddled with his tripod and another camera. His telescopic lense was huge and he wore a national geographic hat, so clearly he was a big deal, or at least in his eyes. Unfortunately, one guide didn't understand that having the most expensive equipment meant the American had the right to push anyone he wanted out of the way. After all, he had paid more for his camera. A man with 3 cameras and another one in his hands, is clearly above all laws and should be treated as such. '*Move*' he barked at the guide standing in front of him, before again telling him to '*move move move, it's my shot*'. The guide stepped back. The American placed his tripod down and continued shooting. The guide naturally annoyed confronted him, ' *I'm standing here, you can't just tell me to* move. *Don't be so rude'*. The man looked up for half a second with an expression simultaneously managing to be taken aback by being spoken to and also being completely disinterested in what he had to say, grunted and went back to his camera. I looked over at the guide and said don't mind him and then cursed the American in Nepali, under my breath in a pathetic show of solidarity. The guide smirked.

I wondered what it was about seeing big animals that so often turned rational human beings so irrational but I couldn't put my finger on it. I was sure it was something to do with having a story to tell, this made people, I'm sure, claim they saw a tiger when deep down they know they didn't. I had seen this all over the world. People arguing over the best view, or place to take a photograph, normally when animals were involved. I recalled a literal traffic jam in Kruger National Park in South Africa, over spotting a leopard. Arguments had soon broken out from people stuck at the back of the queue and startled by the commotion the leopard had soon scarpered. Seemingly rational people who were content to sit for hours waiting for an animal, lost all sense and semblance of patience when the animal actually came near and in that moment emotions often ran high.

It was then that I heard the photographer speak to his guide in broken Nepali, and glower at me. He'd probably heard me, and more importantly, knew what I had called him. At least he wasn't staying at my resort. Ten minutes after the tiger arrived it left turning back into the jungle. We all did the same, just in our case most people were looking for their respective jeeps.

That night on return to my empty resort, I found that it, in fact, was no longer empty. Amongst the shrubbery outside the dining room stood a buffalo carcass, strung up on a tree in the middle of being cut and gutted. Around it stood around 10 Scandinavians and at least 40 Nepalese. It turned out the group was a television crew, filming a form of survival show inside Bardia and they had wanted to have a BBQ. Not being satisfied with chicken, they instead decided to buy a buffalo. Buffalos cost around twenty to twenty-five thousand rupees, depending on the size. The Scandinavians were attempting to butcher it themselves, and while to my untrained eye they seemed to be doing a decent job, their attempts were accompanied by much mirth from the locals. After watching for a few minutes I decided to remove myself from all the flies that had congregated around the carcass and instead continued my new routine of sitting and drinking warm beer.

I sat near the entrance of the dining room under a tree and as I drank my beer I watched as half the village arrived into the resort all clutching little plastic bags. When invariably they would leave after 30 seconds their bags full of buffalo meat I had to laugh. I laughed even harder after speaking to Suresh. I'd asked him how much meat you could get from a buffalo, and how much meat these guys would get for their twenty-five thousand. Apparently, they thought that they would get around fifteen to twenty kilos and then would give the rest away. Therefore everyone, Suresh included, was on the phone telling their friends to come and get some free meat. Although I almost laughed even harder when speaking to some of the Scandinavians, I again asked how much meat they were expecting to get from their buffalo. When one of them replied only around five kilos or more, it was all I could do to contain my laughter. At almost $250 for those five kilos of meat, that was one expensive BBQ.

Western Terai

The next day it was time to head further west so I left Bardia behind and got on a bus to Nepalgunj, one of the largest and most important cities in west Nepal. The journey took four hours in the morning heat and the bus had stopped the normal excruciating amount of times on the way. After arriving I was looking forward to walking around for a while before finally having a cold beer. Yet it had to be said that there wasn't a huge amount easily accessible to do to kill a few hours until the evening. I wandered around the town, although with it mainly consisting of several busy straight roads with shops either side and just one or two roundabouts to break up the monotony of the straights, and with the heat bearing down I quickly tired of that idea.

There were, however, some of the largest mosques I had seen in Nepal lining the streets, so I tried unsuccessfully to enter a few; without exception, they were all locked. I did find one with a security guard, so I asked the man behind the gate if I could come in. He shook his head. I realised afterwards when looking back that as the Terai is a big homeland of the Nepali Christian movement, a successful version at that, with Nepal having one of the highest conversion rates in the world, I could easily have been mistaken for a missionary. This may well be why I wasn't allowed to enter. Having seen some awful behaviour by missionaries before in Nepal, entering a mosque in an attempt to convert people, was not actually as implausible as it first sounded.

After a short uneventful night's stay in Nepalgunj, I hopped on another bus and headed further west, to Dhangadi. The small micro that sped along the East-West Highway took three hours dodging tractors, schoolkids, bicycles and oversized lorries coming from India before we screeched to a halt in Dhangadi.

There is even less to say for Dhangadi, as far as tourists or visitors are concerned at least, than Nepalgunj. After finding a ticket counter and securing my ticket I had several hours to kill. I wandered the streets for a bit, before again quickly tiring of the same sights. I really needed a motorbike or at least a bicycle to get around, especially in the heat. In the end, I found a khaja ghar on the side of the road and eat dinner and sink some beers. I tried to call a few friends as I know the signal is unlikely for the next few weeks, but I couldn't get through. So I continued to drink, read and listen to other people's conversations. Two young guys are returning to Surkhet after working in India, an elderly couple are returning home after seeing their son and grandson in the Terai. Being a transport hub most people are on the move and few were actually from Dhangadi. Then having killed a few hours it was time to head over to the bus station in Attarai.

Attarai is situated on the East-West Highway, a convenient jumping off point for buses headed north. As Dhangadhi is a couple of kilometres south from the highway I got back on a bus and headed back up the road I had come down just a few hours ago. Getting off at the bus park, it was clear this dusty park was the main, and only, draw of the town. Wandering around my first impressions were that this was a bit rougher than other places I'd been, with the unmistakeable air of yet another transit town, everyone coming and going with no-one staying. Apart from its location on the highway, there was little to offer but food, drink and some dusty streets. And certainly no attractions

I went to the ticket counter where they checked my ticket for the 5 pm bus to Darchula which was due to arrive around 7 am the next day. One of the guys gestured to the rocky berth it would pull into and then told me that the bus had been delayed in its departure by an hour and a half. I was by now incredibly used to, and resigned to this and sat and waited. Yet after an hour or so I asked the ticket seller when the bus was supposed to be leaving. *'Ah Bhai, there is a diesel shortage and the bus is in the queue. It should be here in the next 30 minutes'*

'Maybe 30 minutes, maybe 1 hour?' I replied

'Maybe Maybe, we'll have to wait and see' he replied laughing.

So I went to get a cup of tea and stretch my legs, still merely passing the time.

An hour after the revised and delayed departure time the bus finally rolled into view, yet the crowd of people surrounding the bus seems smaller than usual. Even after all the bags are loaded on and passengers have gotten on, it was still well under-capacity. This is certainly not the norm for a long distance bus, which would normally wait a painfully long amount of time after the departure time has passed to fill all remaining seats up before departing, and then stopping every 20 metres to collect yet another passenger. Maybe not this time. Maybe travelling in the far-west was easier than I had heard. What had all my friends moaned about? It was then that the rest of the passengers arrived.

Normally goats ride in the privileged, and much-envied position of the roof, where there is more room, a better view, a breeze in summer and most importantly, an escape route. If anything happened to a bus, inside packed like sardines there's nothing you can do. At least on the roof, you can entertain the fantasy of jumping off last minute before the bus plunges into a ravine. Yet today for some reason, the bags were all on the roof. Even small backpacks were forced on the roof. I found out why minutes later when ten goats boarded the bus. Filling up the aisle they soon made the bus their home by grazing on people's shoelaces or nibbling on seat covers and filling the bus with the smell of wet goat. I wasn't quite sure why the goats were being brought up to the hills from the Terai, as opposed to the other way around. Normally they would be sent down to the market. Not that this question really mattered as soon I had bigger concerns.

The bus, now smelling strong of goat, finally set off at 7pm. Goats normally defecate a lot, which is fine as they are outside and not riding on public transport. These goats, however, were not outside, nor were they used to travelling on buses. Either all 10 goats were suffering from diarrhoea, or they all had simultaneously come down with travel sickness. Within half an hour of leaving the bus station, the floor of the bus was almost underwater. Except it wasn't water, it was diarrhea.

There was one advantage to our now slightly unwelcome fellow passengers. As there were so many goats taking up the back seats I was able to sit in the cabin at the front. When I stuck my head out of the window I could almost stretch out, which also gave a great view of the stars which were incredibly clear, but after repeatedly coming precariously close to walls I soon lost my nerve. Having my head outside did, however, come with an added benefit. The truck's engine was in the front, and the cabin built around it, I rested my feet upon a big box with the engine inside. The heat of the engine grew as we climbed and climbed and the smell of the goatshit only got worse and worse with the heat as the night drew on. We drove for hours climbing up and up the unilluminated hills. Which hill it was and where we were I had no idea as it was dark and the headlights illuminated only a narrow stretch in front of us. The night drew on and the bus clanked its way up to Darchula.

Around 2 am, we reached another unilluminated village and two people got out of the cabin, leaving me with only one other person in the cabin. I could now stretch out without putting my head out of the window. For rural travel, this was definitely luxurious and I thanked my luck.

The driver had been blaring Hindi dance music interspaced with the odd Justin Bieber song throughout the journey, and it was horrible. The music was awful, the speakers were crackly, the sound horribly distorted and it was blasted out at an unfathomably loud volume. After a few hours, I put my headphones in and tried to listen to music in a feeble attempt to drown it out. Yet even with my headphones on full volume, I still couldn't hear anything over the sound of remixed bhangra. This went on for an age until the bus pulled up and the driver popped out for a cigarette when he did that all the other people in the bus were sleeping, so I saw an opportunity and went for it. I reached over and turned the volume level down from 30 to 20, still too loud for the middle of the night, but no longer deafeningly so. Feeling smug I leaned back and shut my eyes. I could hear myself think again. This respite lasted for all of five minutes. When the driver came back, He pulled himself up into his seat, started the engine and then grunted, before leaning over and turning the radio back up to 35. Louder than before

About 3 am we reached Dadledhura and then the bus driver asked me to get out and change bus

'Why?' I asked

'*This bus is going to make lots of stops*'. That bus, he said pointing to a bus in front, '*goes direct and will get you to Khalanga faster.*'

Not really wanting to give up my luxurious front berth but keen to have the journey over and done with I moved my things over and climbed into the other bus. If there were so few people on the other bus, surely there won't be many in this one I thought, walking up the stairs. Only to find the bus crammed full and with no seats left. I perched uncomfortably on the side of a seat for about an hour until someone got off the bus, and I was finally able to get a seat next to an older man who promptly fell asleep on my shoulder, his snores rasping in my face. At least there were no animals in this bus

I awoke around 5 the next day with a start. The sun was already streaming down and for the first time since leaving the plains, I had an idea of where I was. Looking out of the window, I immediately wished I hadn't. Overnight the roads had deteriorated massively and often had areas where the road simply disappeared. This was normal due to Nepal's topography. Having travelled on my fair share of buses and bikes in Nepal I felt I was used to this. But this was different. Immediately to my left, the road fell away for a good few hundred metres. On its own, this was just about bearable. But the road surface had also given away to gravel track littered with broken down buses and lorries. Flying past them we climbed up passes and shot back down the other side of the pass. Only to turn a corner into the next valley to do the same thing. The drops were bigger than any I'd seen before, this on what was a relatively major road towards a district headquarters. Nepal has its fair share of dangerous roads. There are numerous accidents and most highways involve some precarious cliffs or passing places. But the drop-offs here were unparalleled. In some places you could see 500, 600 metres below where there was a small river, almost mockingly winding its way safely down the valley.

As the day fully began to break, the bus started to stop along the way and picked up more passengers to fill the aisles and foot wells. The person now sitting next to me, a farmer of around 30 had been chewing paan relentlessly over the last hour. He had suddenly started to look rather pale. All of a sudden he grabbed my shoulder with a sense of urgency, opened the window and started producing an ungodly sound from his mouth, hacking up paan and phlegm over me and some out of the window. This left a brown stain down the outside of the bus and a smaller stain inside on the window sill and on my trousers.

The road itself was poor and our speed had been picking up. What was more, the small concrete barriers on the side of other roads in Nepal, which always threatened to do nothing if a bus actually crashed into them, were missing. Robbed of the small but ultimately meaningless comfort produced by the barriers we carried on.

This monotony of terror went on until at nine that morning, when for the first time I saw the Mahakali River, cutting through the Mahakali valley and acting as the de-facto border between Nepal and India. At this point, the road turned right and we followed the Mahakali north to Khalanga. On the right side, my view was Nepal, to the left of the Mahakali was India only a few hundred metres away. On first impressions, the Mahakali did not seem so big and mighty as its name indicated. The source of the Mahakali is reputed to be at a pond in the Kali temple at Kalapani. A few years ago the Mahakali had swelled to enormous proportions and caused huge damage flooding both the Indian and Nepali side. I remembered watching videos at the time shocked by the size and speed of the river, it seemed truly deserving of its name. However today the wrath of Kali was nowhere to be seen today. Not so much now I thought, a name more like the sanokali, or bisatarikali would be more fitting. As we headed up the river I saw my first glance of a tricolour on the Indian side of the border. They would become ubiquitous as we passed government buildings and private houses, all with the Indian flag. Yet, strangely, on the Nepali side, there was little to no sign of the two pennons that combined to make the distinctive Nepali flag.

Travelling along the border, apart from the slightly higher concentration of Indian flags than usual, there was little to nothing to suggest this was indeed an international border. It was just a river at the bottom of a valley. At least in the Terai, there are the border pillars which even in their haphazard concentration serve to demonstrate the physical location of the border. But here there was nothing, even the signs in India which I could see looked, at the first glance at least, the same, as both Hindi and Nepali use the same Devanagari script.

There were a few government posts and police checkpoints on the Nepali side, with a noticeably higher government presence in towns on the Indian side of the border. But it was obvious that the border is effectively, at night at least, open for anyone. I could, I reckoned, easily cross the border unnoticed from the roadside in a 5 minute run down to, and across the river, and up the river bank again. Flagging down a lift though and passing through Indian checking patrols might be more difficult. Yet clearly it was open and I knew the area had a reputation for being rife with smugglers and being a smuggling hotspot, linking India, Nepal and Tibet and therefore China with amongst other things a lucrative trade in smuggled exotic animal pelts.

It was while I was having my first tentative glances at the Mahakali that I thought about the history of the region and its tumultuous past, characterised by the trans-Himalayan trade and labour migration with many inhabitants of the region arriving whilst escaping persecution from Mughal conquests to the south.

The area I was travelling through was predominately inhabited by the Khas, as well as some Magar and Gurung groups too. The Khas, previously known to as Parbattias or Paharis, now Chettris, were part of the of Khas Malla Kingdom. The whole area I would be travelling through over the next few weeks used to belong to the Khas Empire which spanned from the 11th century to around the 14th. This Kingdom, often under-researched, could boast of immense strength and size. The Khas Kingdom was effectively the area where the predecessors of the later rulers of Gorkha came from as well as where the present day the Nepali language originated, with Devanagari scripts from the 13th century being found inside the boundaries of the former Kingdom. I had read up on the subject however yet found some details of the old kingdom scant and unexpansive.

The Khas Kingdom was large and from its home in the Karnali basin covered current day Uttarakhand, large swathes of Western Nepal and parts of southwestern Tibet. This empire would soon grow into one of significant importance. The empire, according to Whelpton would grow to become 142,000 square kilometres and the rulers had long been noticed for their raids into the Kathmandu valley.

Life in the Khas Empire was potentially the high point for Darchula and the Western Hills and after the breakup of the Empire at the end of the fourteenth and the beginning of the fifteen century, their glory would struggle to be heard over the unification and conquests of the later Gorkha Kingdom.

In his controversial book, Fatalism and Development, Dor Bahadur Bista, provides an overview and critique of the Khas Empire, which lasted from the eleventh century to the sixteenth century. According to Bista,

"The Khas state did not develop a flourishing urban centre of art and luxury as the Newars had done. They maintained their martial prowess with a simple lifestyle, largely determined by the area they occupied."

The mainstay of the Khas economy was the cultivation of wet rice in their river valleys. However this relatively sparse and frugal empire did not last forever, and Bista blames the introduced of a strict Hierarchical Hinduism

"The Empire initially patronised Buddhism. With the introduction of the hierarchic caste system and fatalistic faith, Khas society, too, began to ossify and by the sixteenth century the western Khas Empire disintegrated."

When reading I tried to understand the complex history behind names, without much luck. Despite these few extracts, there was however not exactly a wealth of literature surrounding the Mahakali valley, Darchula or the Khas. Many of the extracts or texts that I did manage to find in English tended to often have contradictory statements or use different names for languages and ethnic groups. Khas and Khasa infrequently occur in place names in Western and Central Asia, leading some to believe they originated there long ago before travelling to South Asia. Bista dates them arriving at the western flanks of Nepal at around the beginning of the first millennium BC.

Some believe that the name for the Khas or Khasa has its origins in the Nepali verb Khas, meaning to fall. Therefore the insinuation is that the Khas is a fallen tribe. Jung Bahadur Rana also re-labelled the Khas as Chettri, and many have renamed themselves Chettri to avoid the stigma of the noun's connotations and as a result, the term Khas has almost become redundant in Nepal. Although the term Khas in Nepal has now almost become obsolete, as a result of their history Khasa people can take pride in a strong, if confusing and slightly mixed up the historical lineage

I was still a little confused about the history this morning on the highway. The only thing I could be sure of today was that is an area of historic migration. By now we had bumped our way alongside the Mahakali for several hours and at 10.30 the bus mercifully finished limping through the old Khas Kingdom and into pulled Khalanga Bazaar.

Khalanga

I got off the bus and slightly staggering under the weight of my 4 bags, walked the five hundred metres or so from the bus park into town. There was a lot of construction going on by the banks of the river, still repairing the damage done by the floods several years ago. Khalanga is situated on the banks of the Mahakali, with the river on the left and hills stretching up immediately around it. The town across on the other side is also called Darchula, but this time in the Indian State of Uttarakhand. Walking through the narrow concrete streets there is a dense concentration of shops and all the usual familiarities of a bazaar town in the hills. Nothing particularly unique, apart from the slightly larger concentration of goats, cows, buffalo and dogs roaming around than usual for a district headquarters.

I found a hotel, the Hotel Prince, which happened to be located directly opposite the district court. I asked for a room and a girl of about fifteen got the ring of keys from behind the door and walked up the stairs.

She asked me, what country I was from in Hindi,

'*Ah, I don't speak Hindi, only Nepali*' I explained.

'*Not a problem*' she replied switching to Nepali.

I explained where I was from and what I was doing to a disinterested teenager, she murmured her apparent approval in response.

She led me to a small room, completely identically to most other hotel rooms in Nepal. I asked how much, '*600 rupees*' she replied. '*But if you want a hot shower and a TV we have one for 800 rupees*'. Considering it might be my last hot shower for a long while, we walked upstairs to the deluxe room. Which was identical apart from a shower, a western toilet as opposed to the squat toilet and a TV. After the girl left I turned the shower on to let the water warm up and while I was waiting I tried the TV. It turned on, but there was no signal. Looking behind the TV, there was only a power cable attached and no sign of a TV cable at all which rendered it effectively useless. At least I could have a hot shower. Yet the water remained cold for 20 minutes and remained that way until I gave up waiting for it to heat up. From my window, I could see down into the courtyard of the district court. Two policemen were standing talking while another sat on a chair near the entrance to the court while two old dogs lay down nearby. Not much was going on there either. Feeling tired, cold and miserable I lay down on the bed to take a nap only for the noise blaring from a shop next door to keep me awake.

Walking around Khalanga later that day, it became immediately clear that the border is the main driver behind the town's trade and business. Sitting down in a khaja ghar drinking overly sweetened tea I watch porter after porter walk past. Men, women and some children carrying everything from cement, sweets, food, oil, and cigarettes walked hurriedly past in a never-ending stream to and from the border. The shops nearby had everything you could need, from televisions, jewellers, barbers from India, thick coats from China and then the usual beauty shops, butchers, vegetable stalls, electronic

Photo 3: Khalanga Bazaar and the bridge to India

shops that you find in any village in the South Asian hills. There were also several shop lots empty apart from huge piles of wood. There were many around. It was clear that firewood is a major source of energy. I had read beforehand that most households in Darchula rely on wood and the Chulo, a type of traditional stove, and this seemed to confirm it. I thought back to the piles of wood on the roadside on the way to Khalang and I now knew their eventual destination.

The border itself is a metal suspension bridge with police checking on both sides. There is no international visa processing here, so the border is only open to Nepalese and Indians. The police on the Nepali side at least, about six in total, sat around in determined disinterest. Drinking tea and staring at their phones, with the occasional half-hearted look in someone's bag, the border seemed lax enough.

I did approach the border, although I knew I wouldn't be allowed
. across. I remembered almost 4 years ago, as an intern in Nepal I had
travelled to Kodari and the Friendship Bridge at the border between
Nepal and Tibet in Sindhupalchowk. While then I had been able,
after asking the security guards, to walk out onto the bridge and
technically be in no man's land metres away from Tibet, I didn't have
the same luck this time. The police were happy enough to talk to me
but smiled and laughed before ultimately saying no, I wasn't allowed
on the bridge. Well, as I thought back to me standing on the border
in Kailali, maybe that would have to do for this trip.

The Hotel Prince in addition to the aerial-less television and cold
water also currently lacked a kitchen. So I sat down and had a bowl
of chowmein in a local khaja ghar near the bridge and watched a
steady stream of people cross the bridge. A seemingly never-ending,
a slow but steady stream of people crossed, there was never less than
one person crossing at one time. The chowmein, I noticed, had also
been cooked on a wooden stove.

The inhabitants all seemed to me to either be Nepali or Indians
from Uttarakhand and there were not as many Tibetans as I had
thought. I heard a mixture of Hindi, Nepali and Khas, the local
dialect. One language I didn't hear was English, and it was clear the
town didn't attract too many inquisitive Englishmen by the reaction
I was getting. Several old men stopped me in the street and asked me
where I was from and we had pleasant enough conversations. Very
few of these old men, I couldn't help but notice had any front teeth
left. But later several groups of younger boys had in a mocking tone
asked me if I was American, and then seemed to barely be able to ask
if I was *'having the good time'* before bursting into laughter. They
managed to combine curiosity and hostility all into a three-second
exchange.

I thought back to the things I had read and heard about Darchula
being a hot spot for pelt and skin trading, as well as smuggling. There
was, in some places and amongst some people, a real rough border

town attitude to the place that frankly wasn't so endearing. This was backed up by the ominous placement of numerous scars on the local's arms, hands and faces; it was easy to see how Darchula got its bad reputation. Being situated literally a stone's throw away from India, I could see how this place could well attract people wanting to escape from the hands of security forces on either side of the border.

Traditionally, Darchula was part of an area famed for its role in the Trans-Himalayan trade, which was essential to the Khasa Empire. Tibetan salt was by far the most in-demand commodity, alongside mules, goats, donkeys and wool. In return, Nepal would send rice and copper to the north and onwards to Lhasa. Rice, unable to be grown at such high altitude was particularly sought after. Inside the Khasa Kingdom, two major passes to Tibet resided inside its territory. Both were to the east of Darchula. According to Pradhan

> "The two main routes lie on the banks of the two tributaries of the Karnali river, system, the Mugu Karnali and the Humla Karnali. These routes were within the Khasa kingdom and were later controlled by the Kalyal chiefs of Jumla. From the Humlis in the west to the Sherpas in the east, the frontier tribes exploited the geographical situation between the Tibetan highlands and the lower regions of Nepal, making good use of their ability to transport goods across higher altitudes."

While the major routes to Tibet in the region were situated to the east of Darchula, such as through the Mugu and Humli Karnali, the famed Limi salt traders did pass through Darchula on their way to Lhasa.

This trade flourished until the arrival of cheaper Indian manufactured salt, which became popular and undercut the Tibetan monopoly of the salt trade. Today, however, the northern frontier regions of Nepal retain the feel of places of geographical and cultural exchange. These days there is no sign of the famed Limi traders and now most trade is done with India instead, with the Yak caravans to Lhasa a long distant memory. Now instead lorries and trucks dealt with the new trade of gems, electronics, materials and clothes, a far cry from salt from Manasarovar. The porters coming over the border laden with goods are all that remains of this famous trading route.

After an hour or so of walking around and around the bazaar with night now approaching I headed back to my hotel, wanting a drink, but not wanting to drink alone in a bar, as I knew there was no way I would be allowed to sit in silence reading a book, so I grabbed two bottles from a shop and went back to my room. The watering holes I passed were already echoing with the sound of drunken revelry by the time I reached my hotel.

At night Khalanga really came to life. By that, I meant from around 9 pm until midnight the streets were full of noises. I could hear shouting, bottles breaking, phones ringing and the sound of the all too ubiquitous dogs barking and fighting. I was particularly glad I wasn't outside drinking. At around 10:30 pm, one dog in particular which had been barking for a good fifteen minutes all of a sudden started to yelp continuously which was followed by the low pitch laughter of an old drunken man. I reckoned he must have been throwing stones at the dog, initially to shut then it up, but got a little carried away. The dog must have been trapped in a corner unable to escape. Later when at midnight the noises finally died down, I realised just why so people many had scars on their faces.

The next day I called Narayan, the man who would be my guide, fixer and interpreter of Khas on the trip and we arranged to meet up later in the day. I had heard there were a number of NGO's in the area and I had planned to spend the day speaking and interviewing people for my thesis and hopefully make some contacts and gather information. Yet there wasn't nearly as many as I thought. What's more, it turned out the NSU elections were taking place soon and the town had become host to several protests and rallies which not only were a major source of distraction for everyone, it meant several of the offices I went to were closed. Giving up, I went back and had another bowl of chowmein again and waited to meet up with Narayan.

I met Narayan in the late afternoon and we went for tea. He was a tall lanky Nepali, a Baral, and lived up in Dailekh, just an hour or so from Khalanga. Over tea, he told me about his family and three kids, who lived in Mahendranagar for school and for work. We outlined the route for the trek and sorted everything we would need to take.

We spent what was left of the evening drinking beer and pouring over our maps. Yet we had a small issue. On my trekking map, everything was in English, but the map was not very detailed and over thirty years old. Being in English it meant Narayan couldn't read it very well. I had another updated local district map, which was in Devanagari, which he could read, but I couldn't. Of all the luck.

Dailekh

The next day our aim was to reach Dailekh a small town an hour or two away from Khalanga by jeep. Once there we would rest for the night before setting off on our trek early the following morning. Narayan was from Dailekh and was naturally excited to be going home and seeing his daughter Anu, the only member of his family not living in Mahendranagar.

During my stay the National Student Union, or N.S.U, elections had been taking place, or at least some vigorous campaigning was going on. Often in Khalanga, I would be disturbed from wandering aimlessly around the bazaar, or from hanging around the border, hoping some gallant border policeman would take an interest in me, and eventually let me on the bridge, by the shouts and cries of around a hundred students. At least two students carrying large speakers shouting out, often accompanied by a large amount of static, about politics and the need to make a stand about something. Although due to the static and accompanying drums it was almost impossible to hear what the actual protestors were demanding. Staying in one place for an hour, you would inevitably see the protest return two or three times, which robbed the protests of some anger and led instead to a slightly farcical air to proceedings. At least the crowded streets prevented the motorbike rallies from entering the town, leaving them to ply the outskirts of Khalanga instead. It was a relatively small town after all with few places to properly congregate, so the protests would march in elongated circles through the already tight and narrow streets. If nothing else, it provided a nice distraction from the monotony of just hanging around the bazaar and waiting to leave.

We had agreed to meet at 1 pm which gave me yet again some more time to kill in the bazaar. I bought a torch, some matches, spare batteries and a couple of packs of biscuits and noodles to eat on the way. Having exhausted the sights and shops of the bazaar yet again, I decided to do what I did most times in Nepal when I found myself with time to kill. I went to the barber for a shave and head massage. Getting a straight blade dragged across my face and having my head vigorously rubbed, if nothing else, is an easy way of passing twenty minutes. Then after having some rice and curry, I went back to my hotel to have a cold bucket shower, the hot water was apparently still heating up from last night. I lay down and tried to read my book. I'd brought along an eccentric collection, from a textbook on Maoism and the cultural practices of Maoists in Nepal, a few assorted histories of Nepal and Kipling's Plain Tails of the Hills which I was re-reading. I settled on the Kipling and waited until it was time to meet Narayan.

We met up later on and picked our way through the bazaar to the north of Khalanga and the trailhead to Dailekh. There were four Mahindra jeeps parked haphazardly in a rocky clearing, one jeep had its bonnet raised and there was a man working underneath it. Narayan spoke to him, asking about when the next jeep would leave to Dailekh. The man replied coarsely that they were all booked, and we hadn't made a reservation. I was surprised, this didn't seem like it was such a high flying operation to require a ticket reservation system. Narayan and the submerged mechanic argued for another thirty seconds or so before the man drew back from under the jeep. He wasn't a man at all, just a boy of around fourteen who seemingly from smoking a lot had the sounds and tone of a much older man. Despite being covered in mud and oil from lying on the wet ground, Narayan took him away by his arm and they walked away out of earshot having a whispered conversation. When they returned only minutes later Narayan told me the jeep would be leaving in five minutes and we would indeed be on it. He never told me what it exactly was that he said. This wouldn't be the last time I would see Narayan use his persuasive skills to our advantage.

Eventually the jeep, now crammed full with elderly villagers returning home from the bazaar, and I and Narayan set off. The road wound its way away from Khalanga climbing steeply and heading east, back away from the border. When looking back, with our new found height we could see all the way over the Indian hills and into the Uttarakhand Himalayas. They dominated the skyline for a few moments until we passed into another valley and after dropping down they were behind us and no longer in sight.

We picked up a couple of locals for a few kilometres or so who regardless of age hung, or rather dangled off the side. It felt great to be finally on the road, after months of planning and days of travel. There was, I always felt, an air of the unknown about any big trip in Nepal, of whether despite planning it would actually happen. The road was as equally hazardous as the day before and, in some places worse due to heavy mud on sharp corners. Yet being in a small jeep, and with no other traffic, I was able to relax and watch the fields and rivers go by. We passed yet more bundles of wood along the roadside. While Dailekh does have a new community forest, other wood was seemingly more easily accessed and readily available for harvest. I was able to spot small trails up seemingly impossibly steep hillsides and people at work on the farms for the 2 hours it took to reach Dailekh. Around this area, houses are few and far between, often with big distances between houses in the settlement. The typical house often had the upper story for people and lower story for cattle, a few terraces and a little plot of land. Chickens, goats and children,

Photo 4: Dailekh, Narayan's hometown, with the Indian Himalayas in the background

all equally filthy would ubiquitously be running around lost for something to do.

Dailekh is a small settlement in Khar VDC. It proudly boasts a small police post, a few tea shops, and a school for lower primary students and surprisingly despite consisting only of a few hundred inhabitants, a dilapidated branch of Janata bank. It lies on the ridge of a valley, to the right you can gaze right into the hills of Nepal and left, although often covered by cloud, lies the Uttarakhand Himalayas and in the far distance Nanda Devi National Park. Looking down into Khar valley, you see the valley fall away in front of you. It drops for several hundred metres, the drop consisting of hills, terraces and patchy forest. Being on a ridgeline, it was noticeably cooler and I longed for Khalanga's envious wind protection, being nestled at the valley bottom. As I walked around the town, there were a few new houses being constructed, using the traditional method of brick coated in mud and straw for insulation, before the top half is painted white and the bottom a rusty orange. There was, a beautiful lack of corrugated tin sheeting as used for roofs. While an undoubtedly useful material for building a roof, tin roofing is as hideously ugly as it is noisy and a poor insulator. The extent of tin roofing in Nepal, which was already high before the earthquake, skyrocketed after the earthquake. There was an obvious rationale behind it and it did make a lot of sense, but that didn't stop the new tin-roofed buildings from being an eyesore, while the older traditionally roofed buildings remained elegant in comparison. In so many places traditional building methods were being lost in the rush to adopt imported techniques and materials. If nothing else it is nice to be reminded of the simple elegance of these older houses.

Looking down to the Mahakali and the border, the abstractness of the division hits home. While using a river, and a large sacred one at that, as a border does make some sense, it does also seem slightly ridiculous. To have one Sovereign territory one side of a large stream and another on the other seems to make a lot more sense in academic discussions where the border is an arbitrary yet highly discussed line on a map than it does in the flesh. If the river changed its path did the physical boundaries of the border follow the river or instead did they remain static and lie on the old course of the river? What sheer nonsense. Has the current trajectory of the Mahakali changed at all since when it was demarcated as the border in 1816, and if so, who had gained territory and who had lost territory?

While doing some background reading I found several references in some slightly more obscure literature. In an old faded battered, but first edition copy, of famed Nepali scholar Harka Gurung's collection of travelogues I found the following mentions of Darchula and the Mahakali Valley.

"The hills of the Mahakali Zone are inhabited entirely by Brahmin, Thakuri, Chettri and numerous occupational castes. Baitadi indeed forms a bridge between Kumaon and Garhwal on one hand and west Nepal hills between the Mahakali and Karnali on the other and the whole area has a common historical and cultural heritage' Harka Gurung found that, *'In spite of the establishment of the Mahakali river as the boundary between Nepal and British India after the Anglo-Nepalese war since 1816, the area on either side of the Mahakali still form a single cultural entity with similar caste structure, popular religion, art and architecture."*

This made sense as before the British-Gurkha wars of 1814-16, the Gorkha kingdom stretched out much further west than just to the Mahakali. With its dominion including both Kumaon and Garwhal, the western edge of the Kingdom extended up to the Sutlej River and the edges of the Punjab. Yet after 1816 and the Sugauli treaty all territory west of the Mahakali became East Indian Company territory, then part of British India before being incorporated into the Republic of India in 1947. I stared into what once was part of the old Gorkhali Kingdom.

With not a lot else to do, we went for tea. The house again had a chulo, and the wall behind it was thick black with soot. As the young man in charge, who couldn't have been over thirty, stoked the fire he hacked and coughed his guts up, placed the pot of milk on top of it and waited for it to boil. I felt I could safely assume the colour of the wall matched that of his lungs. With heavy levels of smoking and soot inhalation inherent in the use of chulos, it was hardly surprising cases of COPD were so common here and other rural areas of Nepal. As we had tea we started talking, his name was Ashish and he lived above the teashop. He was a Tribhuvan University graduate he said, of English literature. I sat amazed as he started talking about Shakespeare and the poetry of Keats and Wordsworth, all the while stoking the fire. I couldn't help wondering when the last time the English literature curriculum, in all probability based on an old Benares Hindu University or Jawaharlal Nehru University curriculum was updated. Forcing students, especially in a country with dubious standards of English particularly in government schools, to read dusty old tomes of English literature and poetry just seemed cruel if nothing else. How relatable were the old romantic poets to school children in England these days, let alone in the Western Himalayas. But now, he said, there were no opportunities for him so when he finished his bachelors, this was all he could do. His wife worked down the valley in the primary school. He continued to stoke the fire.

I had heard that Darchula was a bit of a Maoist stronghold, yet apart from several fading hammer and sickles daubed onto walls and the odd mural and slogans there appeared no higher Maoist presence than in any other place. There were a number of districts during the Civil War which had been declared class A, where the government presence did not exist outside of district headquarters. Darchula was not one of these, but that being said there didn't seem to be much of a government presence here anyway. I could easily see how inhabitants could find sympathy with the Maoists, or at least their theories if not their practice. The Maoists were notorious for being as corrupt, nepotistic and more uncouth than the old guard they had overthrown. Darchula was a long way, both physically and mentally, from Kathmandu and the Nepali Government. There was little government investment, neither economic nor rhetorical. Schools and government meetings are conducted in Nepali, not the local Khas dialect. Whenever government officials did come, it was in toe with a huge entourage that only highlighted the differences between the Kathmandu netas and the locals. Being closer to Delhi than to Kathmandu certainly would only highlight or further pronounce these issues. Moreover, when speaking to friends and acquaintances in Kathmandu about the far-west, you'd be forgiven for believing you were embarking on an arduous journey to another country incomparable and far removed from Nepal proper. The people would cheat you, the roads would kill you, there was no proper food and electricity, why, the conversation would invariably end in, why are you going so far and put yourself through such hardship? To travel all that way for any other purpose than financially lucrative work, was almost unfathomable. The disconnect then was real. The Far-West for many who had not been remained the Wild West.

Later I met the porter, Ramji. He was a fifty-year-old skinny man, who never went anywhere without his topi. Yet immediately when introducing myself I find myself struggling to understand what he was saying. Unable to speak Khas, our conversation quickly fizzled out. Had Narayan not been able to come, I clearly would have had issues living in close proximity to someone, and effectively following them, for a week without being able to speak a word. I had been told by a friend in Kathmandu, a senior policeman who had been stationed in Darchula, not to worry as everyone speaks Nepali. He was right, but only in the bazaar. The verbs and nouns were different, as was the pronunciation. While the sentence structure was the same, that didn't help if I didn't know the actual words. I was at a loss and not for the first time on this trip feeling incredibly stupid and unprepared. Would I not be able to have a proper conversation with anyone on this trip?

Yet while Khas was proving a hurdle it was historically instrumental in founding what constitutes modern-day Nepali. While present-day Khas, may be considered a local dialect and now different from the Nepali spoken today, it formed the basis for the modern-day Nepali. Following the replacement of Newari with Khas Kura after the Gorkhas conquests of Kathmandu, it was Khas which became the official language of the Nepali state. The Khasa amidst their military campaigns travelled and spread out from Western Nepal all over the country from Central to Eastern Nepal and took their language with them.

Khas Kura spread like wildfire through the hills of Nepal. A source at the time, Dr Francis Hamilton while while visiting between 1802 and 1803 and who would go onto write one of the first histories of Nepal, noted that

> *"the language spoken by the mountainous Hindus, in the vicinity of Kathmandu is usually called the Parbatiya Bhasa or mountain dialect; but west from the capital, it is more commonly known by the name of Khas Bhasa, or dialect of the Khas country, because it seems to have been first introduced into the territory of that name…There can be no doubt that it is a dialect of the Hindi (sic) language, and it is making rapid progress in extinguishing the aboriginal dialects of the mountain."*

The later Shah dynasty of the Gorkha Kingdom spoke the Khas Bhasa. Yet as the Khas's social status was seen to be inferior when compared to the incoming Rajput's many people instead claimed Rajput ancestry. Interestingly enough, even Jung Bahadur Rana attempted to distance himself from his Khas roots, when he decreed that Gorkhali should be the new term to describe the lingua franca of Nepal, instead of Khas Bhasa. Yet as British administrators had adopted the term Nepal, from either Newar or Nepa as in Banepa, the language eventually became known, as it is today, as Nepali.

Yet knowing that Nepali descended from Khas wasn't of much practical use at the time, in fact, it made not being able to communicate even more frustrating, as it seemed despite Nepali originating from Khas, it had clearly changed a lot further from the original. Not understanding the dialect was like having cataracts, only the rough outlines of topics and opinions would reveal themselves to me, it was beyond frustrating.

I couldn't help feeling a little uncomfortable when speaking to Ramji. I was feeling a mixture of guilt and laziness for hiring a porter. I could carry the load myself, it would just take me an extra few days

I didn't have. I had never used a porter before on previous trekking trips, much preferring to struggle on with an overloaded backpack in a misguided attempt to gain respect from people I didn't know. Yet in many ways, me not hiring a porter out of moral indignation was ridiculous. Had I not stayed in lodges in rural areas completely constructed by materials brought by porters? Had I not eaten food and drunken beer at lodges where every morsel was solely bought up by porters? Was, therefore, my moral righteousness the same as a meat eater who doesn't like to watch the animal they are about to eat being killed? I was prepared to overlook someone's hardships when they were hidden, so why couldn't I stare them in the face? The overwhelming majority of work for porters in Nepal is domestic, not relating to trekkers or tourism. Although I did wonder whether any guilt pangs would emerge later on when climbing. Certainly when on previous trekking trips I'd never felt the urge to carry any extra weight. I passed off my guilt with a decent daily wage and an endless supply of cigarettes to Ramji. He didn't touch alcohol but his dedication and persistence to his smoking habit was almost impressive.

I looked over at Narayan, he was dressed in a collared shirt, corduroys and a pair of trainers. I looked down at my £200 walking boots, branded walking trousers and expensive jacket and felt a wave of embarrassment. Knowing it had snowed recently I had packed extensively, rather too extensively I now felt. Seeing most women and men in Dailekh walk around in chappals, I wish I hadn't bothered. I thought back to growing up in the Lake District in northern England, making fun of ramblers and tourists with hundreds of dollars of equipment to walk along a path that was almost wheelchair accessible, and felt I was on the outside looking in. Thinking critically, my 'big trip' was not so remote or grand as I liked to think, but getting carried away with yourself seemed to be a popular pastime in Kathmandu.

That afternoon, over a glass of awful local whisky, or at least that's what the label on the bottle the brown liquid came out of proudly claimed to be, Narayan told me more about the area. It is a hard place to eke out a living. He grew up in Dailekh and told me crops can take 3 months to grow, a comparatively long time, and neither does rice grow up at this altitude. Numerous locals travel abroad, not to the Gulf or Saudi as is so popular elsewhere in Nepal, but rather to India to work as day labourers. The local schools were apparently and understandably not very good, with Narayan's three out of his four kids studying in English medium school in Mahendranagar, a good, or bad, 20 hours by bus from Dailekh. Narayan's ruminations, however, were soon interrupted when an old lady entered the Khaja ghar. Her clothes had turned almost to rags, her hair was thick with knots and she waved a metal plate around while murmuring incomprehensively. She clearly was suffering from long-term mental illness. I asked Narayan what was wrong, he replied that she was *bahulo*, crazy, After walking around the room banging her plate on whatever she could find, the man who'd served us the whisky stood up from the fire, came over to the old lady and started shouting at her and waving at her to go outside. After he continued shouting at her, for what seemed far too long, she slowly walked out of the room, not before he'd snatched the metal plate out of her hand. Knowing how much importance is placed on your elders in Nepal, particularly in rural areas, I felt rather shocked how a man who must have been in his early thirties could be so rude and effectively shoo an elderly mentally deranged person out of his shop. Only for him to then take the plate over to the fire, and fill it full of rice and dhal and then take it outside to the women, who was now screaming at a, under the circumstances, very relaxed dog. Immediately I began to feel guilty for accusing, luckily only in my head, the man for being so brusque and dismissive and for not giving him the benefit of the doubt. I plagued my guilt by asking him questions. It turned out she was the man's grandmother and she had been *bahulo* for as long as anyone could remember. There was a lack of understanding of mental illness in Nepal, not just in rural areas, but here I had mistaken a lack of understanding for a lack of compassion. As I left the room, she was cleaning her plate with a rock.

That night, no longer in the foodless Prince hotel in Khalanga, I stayed in one of the more obscure places I had stayed in for quite some time. In Dailekh there is a small ANCA outpost office, and maybe fifteen metres behind that was a meeting hall. The hall was constructed and paid for by GIZ and then donated to ANCA. The hall contained one large meeting room, with posters and advertisements of NGOs littering the walls, yet adjoining it was a small bedroom. The hall was apparently designed to play host to ANCA meetings, but as indicated from a closer inspection of the dust-covered garbage bin in my room, played host more to late night drinking sessions by the empty cigarettes packets and empty bottles of booze left around. The bedroom was designed to allow ministers and officials from out of town to stay in what is in Darchula relative luxury. There was even a semi-plumbed in the toilet. When it hit 7 pm, the power from the nearby generator kicked in lighting up the room, and all the other houses. The light luckily revealed no nasty surprises.

That evening me Narayan and Bharat, another employee of ANCA, sat down in the meeting hall to drink more imitation whisky. It was almost palatable when drowned in hot water. Narayan had asked for some chicken, but there was none available at a price he was willing to pay. That was not a problem, however, as he merely reached under the desk and pulled out a filthy white plastic bag containing dried fish, which he sent down to his house for his daughter to fry for us. As we ate the fish and I drank the whisky, Bharat told me he too had all his family, including five children down in Mahendranagar. Later on, he told me that he'd been working for

ANCA for five years and was waiting until the local elections before his post would be changed. The local elections were due to be held in a few months. Considering local elections hadn't taken place for 20 years, all talk was on the elections and who would win. It was currently a UML district and Nepali Congress had been campaigning hard, but most people assumed the Maoists would win. The night passed congenially enough until Narayan and Bharat walked home, and I retired to my meeting hall, determined to enjoy its relative comforts while I could.

The next morning I woke at 5 am up shivering and with a headache, despite my sleeping bag and blankets it was bitterly cold. As I got up and stretched my legs I could see frost on the ground, no wonder I had felt was so cold. That it didn't fill me full of confidence for the camping that was too come. I wandered back to the khaja ghar and ate a bowl of channa and drank some tea while waiting for Narayan to surface.

Jatra

It wasn't long until we set off walking, both me and Narayan collectively cultivating our hangovers. The first hour we walked on a flat path before turning left down into the Khar valley. There passing terraces, goats and cattle the trail dove steeply down. As I picked my way through the rocks, I saw the heavily loaded but rapidly disappearing figure of Ramji scamper ahead. It was a clear day and despite the morning sun and the descent it is cold, but the crisp air offered great visibility of the surrounding valleys. Heading down, I saw a mountain fox scarper along a path to my left. After two hours or so of walking along what was more or less the same terrain, we stopped for tea at a small hut with a few locals sitting around and talking. The man who made us the tea had a baby daughter all of 2 years old, who was running around the courtyard joined by an equally small baby goat. As I sipped my warm overly sweet milk tea I watched the girl pull the goat's hair, unwind its tail and eventually stick her fingers in the goat's eye. This went on for a few minutes until the goat having reached the end of its patience promptly turn around and head-butted the girl, who equally promptly fell over.

Back on our way, the trail started to snake its way uphill again on the left-hand side of the valley. We cross precarious bridges, walk over the remains of landslides and avoid huge drop-offs as we carried on towards Jatra. As we climbed, eagles came flying low over our heads. At one point, had I been armed with a rock I could have hit the eagle with very little effort it was that close. To be able to hear the wind rushing around an eagle as it dove down past us into the gorge below was an experience to behold. Yet as I allowed myself to get carried away with visions of mountaineering and steeling myself with tales of heroism to tell back in Kathmandu, I was promptly overtaken uphill by an old woman wearing chappals, which brought me back down to earth with a crash.

Ramji, as it turned out was fasting. We were coming up to the Hindu festival of Shivaratri. Ramji's mother had passed away 5 years ago and he was preparing for a puja on the morning of Shivaratri, part of his preparation involved fasting which only increased the awe that I had for him and his speed on the hills. We had left on the 22nd February, and Shivaratri was on the 24th, he still had two days of fasting left.

We stopped at a small house above the river for lunch. While we were waiting for lunch Ramji shaved his head and exposed his sikha. The sikha is a small tuft of hair left deferentially on the crown which designates that the person is a Brahmin. As he took off his shirt so Narayan could shave his head, his muscles were exposed. While he had the face of a 60 old man who had lived a hard life, his body was the complete opposite. With no spare body fat, his muscles quietly bulged on his skinny frame, underneath his sacred thread. This explained the apparent ease in which he climbed. As he was being shaved I sat on the floor and watched a buffalo cautiously emerge from under the house as chickens and goats lazily roamed around. I laid back against the wall and shut my eyes for some rest, only to wake up minutes later with a goat nibbling on my boot laces.

Photo 5: Ramji and Narayan heading to Jatra

We ate a filling lunch of dal, rice and ghee. While eating I realised that I had completely forgotten to bring any water purification tablets. Although so far, I had little need for them. Often when stopping for food and eating in someone's home, the only water source was a brass water pot. It would be passed around for you to pour into your mouth with your lips never touching the vessel. It was both communal and a form of deference to caste. Here, with no cups being used, it would be impossible for me to place a water purification tablet in the jug of water without being insulting. What's more, even if I managed to clandestinely slip a tablet it, I'd still have to wait half an hour with the tablet fizzing until it was okay to drink, and have altered the taste, I would be rather unpopular. So far, by drinking from streams and local water I had little to no problems, and despite me managing to overlook a rather crucial item, I did not feel particularly concerned due to the good and clean state of local water sources. Later, I would come to regret my lack of preparation a little more strongly.

After lunch, we continued on our way to Jatra where we would spend the night before heading to Thaisan the next morning. Walking down and gazing around the valley I often stopped when I saw a house, completely isolated high on a hilltop, out of reach from anyone else. I wondered what led people to live so far away when it was clearly several hours walk to the next house, let alone to the shop.

I was struggling to describe the area properly without resorting to worn out tired clichés like unspoilt, untouched, pristine and virgin. Yet it was all of those things. It was hard, however, to reflect on the beauty of the area when everyone that I meet asked about India, the UK or even Kathmandu and the Terai. When so many people want to leave an area due to it being remote and under-developed it seems slightly odd for me to sing the praises about it being the last bastion of the untouched Nepali Himalayas. The very things that bonded and warmed me to the area were the same things that meant a huge proportion of the local populations wanted out. In this light, my, or anyone else's, the romanticism of the area seemed faintly ridiculous.

When we arrived at Jatra in the late afternoon, we found a small settlement at around 2200 metres, which had followed a cruel final ascent. At the end of the trail, we found that the place I had planned to campin was closed. We managed to find a place to stay in the house of the local school keeper and I was given a small storage room with a mattress to sleep in. Narayan and Ramji would sleep with a friend in the next house over. As I went to my room on the ground floor, children would come flocking to my window to point and laugh. This wasn't something I was overly concerned with, although the adults did not appear happy with the so-called intrusion of my privacy. As the teacher closed my window, to stop them looking I sat on my bed, with there being now being no light source, I sat in darkness.

Later on, I heard voices by my door, then more voices. The closed window had not discouraged the children. After a whispered discussion, the door would creep slowly open and in the light from outside, several filthy children stuck their faces through the door and giggled before running away. This would continue to happen several times throughout the evening. Everyone, children aside, had been asking me, what organisation are you from? It's clear not many foreigners come here, and the ones who do are often involved in organisational or developmental work. As a result, people were still curious. Several times when someone asked me where I was from, a nearby friend of theirs would pre-empt my answers. 'He's from South Korea', said one man authoritatively. Another time after having asked where I was from, and me having replied the UK, a man went onto ask me exactly where in Uttar Pradesh, or UP, I was from. In Jatra, an elderly man was convinced I was from Thailand, but 'the Thailand in Europe'. Another man, clearly very proud with his knowledge, told a group that in England, 'most people speak Spanish don't they?' Looking at me for confirmation of his knowledge, and with him being surrounded by his friends, I nodded my consent. These exchanges are repeated here, not to make fun, but rather to demonstrate the lack of exposure to the outside world that still remains.

I think or rather thought, that one reason for this was a lack of television. Many people like to point to tourism as the major driver in exposing Nepalese to the wider world and increasing the depth of their knowledge. I often felt this overlooked what I thought was the most important tool for exposure, the television. Instead of having to read books and imagine Belayat, you could watch moving pictures. Instead of hearing about India from an uncle, you can watch millions cavort around Mumbai every day with Dish-Home. I hadn't really seen any TVs. There was, thinking back, an aerial-less TV in my room in the Hotel Prince back in Khalanga Bazaar. I didn't think that they would be much use without signal.

One thing that had been nagging me so far was how different the area felt, or rather I did. Whilst for obvious reasons I would never blend in amongst Nepalis, I blended into the eclectic mix of westerners who end up stuck in Nepal. Strange foreigners have been accepted in Kathmandu and the surrounding districts at least. Here, however, I felt alien, a feeling rather strange for Nepal. What the main thing this achieved was for me to realise just how few people were coming through the area, and due to the hardships, how few would probably come in in the near future.

That night I bought a rabbit for dinner and sent a young boy over to the next village for beer, as there would be no meat and alcohol for the next 2 days. Yet the rabbit, a cute white floppy thing, was stuck in my room for an hour before dinner. The only reason for this I could assume was for me to bond with an animal right before I would have to eat it. It was a form of test I had to pass that evening. After an hour or so of the rabbit hopping around my room and me studiously trying to ignore it, I was called to the fire outside for dinner. I made sure to take the rabbit with me.

Outside Santosh, the teacher grabbed the rabbit by its ears before promptly breaking its neck and dumping it in a pot of boiling water. After boiling it for 30 seconds we plucked the fur of it before plunging the rabbit hole into the fire. Fortunately, for I was feeling a little guilty, the rabbit was delicious and for four hundred rupees, money well spent.

As I sunk back into my room, shooing away the children who had taken the opportunity of my empty room to, simultaneously both methodically and messily, go through all of my things. Then I was disturbed again, although this time a small boy was pressing two cans of beer into my face. It was Lhasa beer, a beer that was despite the name, very Chinese. The cans were in the remains of a plastic container of 8, clearly, they had been left behind. And given the beer and the location where they had been left was, it was clearly by a

Chinese expedition that had passed through a while ago. It was warm but better than the alternative. I lay back against the wall and drank the beer.

Later at 11 pm while trying to sleep when the children sunk back into my room to gape at the weird ugly white guy, I didn't find it nearly as amusing as I did when it was daylight.

Thaisan

The next day was Shivaratri. Shivaratri, according to Shaivism, was the night when Shiva performs his dance of creation, preservation and destruction, called Tandav. Another legend states it marks the night when Shiva got betrothed to his consort Parvati. Yet for many of the new generation, in Kathmandu at least, it is more commonly associated with Sadhus and smoking weed. It is the one day that the Nepali government effectively deregulates the smoking of marijuana. Either way, Shivaratri was a festival to celebrate and honour Shiva. On the night itself, Shiva is said to manifest himself as a Jyoti linga, or pillar of light. During the evening devotees gather at Shiva mandirs, make offering to the Shiva linga and chant Shiva mantras. The celebrations often continue well into the next few days. It is common for devotees, as in the case of Ramji, to have a fast during Mahashivaratri and to only eat the Prasad left for Shiva.

I woke rather abruptly at quarter to four with Ramji sitting at the end of my bed smoking another of his foul cigarettes. The reason he was up early was for his puja over in Manakot. He set off at around four in the morning, promising to be back around seven, we planned to leave at eight as it was supposed to be a difficult day and with a lot of climbing, we needed the early start. I've always felt its called Shivaratri for a reason, not Shivabihana so getting woken up so early wasn't exactly what I had planned. With a long steep climb up to Thaisan, I felt I would rue the early start later on. But right then I had more pressing issues to deal with. Either the rabbit or the river water had not agreed too well with me.

After going to the toilet I sat and waited for the porter, Narayan had gone ahead to a neighbouring village to secure another porter to carry blankets and cooking equipment then he would and carry on walking ahead. Ramji and I would catch up with him later. Except Ramji didn't return. Seven o clock came and went, as did eight, and nine too. I sat against the wall of the building and yet again watched children run around outside. The time I felt, has much less relevance here. Deadlines have little applicability if you don't look at your watch. Certainly, so far every time that I had asked how long something may take, eke sin, one second, was the standard response, even if the wait might be several hours

At half nine I finally saw Ramji walking slowly back across the other side of the valley. I wasn't too happy yet I knew getting angry would achieve little to nothing, his Puja was for his dead mother after all. When he finally arrived we got busy loading our bags and by ten we set off and immediately started climbing up steep stone rocks cut into the rock. We followed the path of a small river and would follow this path high up before leaving crossing the pass and leaving the valley behind and dropping down Thaisan.

Normally on the trip, there would me, Narayan and Ramji. Yet as we had planned to stay in Thaisan, which due to the temperature at that altitude at this time of year was uninhabited, therefore we had to take another porter, Narvinder Singh, with us to carry food and cooking supplies. Three people effectively working for me, just so I can go on a glorified walk, seemed ever so slightly ridiculous.

The steps had by now given away to a dirt path on top of a series of broken and fractured boulders. Still following the river we dropped into a gorge before starting to climb out of the side of another. Looking back we were rewarded with a stunning view of the hills stretching out beneath us, the snow on the higher hills contrasted sharply with the warm valley floor we could see below. The path we followed now started to deviate from the river and became more erratic and took on an idiosyncratic approach to climbing. After for what appears to be the third time in an hour I climbed steeply for a hundred metres or so only to descend to the same height that I was before. I decided to throw caution to the wind, abandon the path and just follow the riverbank instead, at least there the climbing was gradual. Although as I clamber over boulders and rocks in the river I, not for the first time on my trip, curse my big bulky walking boots. I don't have the feel or precision I need to walk over this terrain and instead of scampering over rocks I feel like I'm trying to ice-skate with a pair of bricks strapped to my feet. I cursed the fact my running shoes, or at this stage, any other pair, are all safely tucked away in my flat in Kathmandu. They also, I reflected, made me stand out even more. Last night around the fire an old man, who I couldn't help but notice only had 3 teeth, was amazed by the sheer size and thickness of the soles of the shoes and he asked me how much I'd paid for them.

'Ah they were an old pair, a gift from a friend', I say trying to redirect the conservation.

'No, but how much money, how many rupees?'

'I don't know' I offered again.

'How many rupees?' The old man repeated with an insistence fuelled by curiosity.

Realising I was in fact just prolonging the awkward encounter I gave in. 'Um around 10,000 rupees', I said sheepishly, halving the actual figure

'So expensive!', gasped the man, and I realised not for the first time I was wearing over a month's wages on my feet. Or rather more accurately on each foot.

Photo 6: Narayan walking through the meadows

From Jatra you could see snow nestled in the woods of the higher hills, I wondered if we would encounter snow, and realised while a light footfall would be nice, I wasn't really prepared or equipped to spend several days camping in a snow storm.

The path from Jatra to Thaisan entered a small forest and the river was by now growing ever smaller and becoming increasingly made up of frost. I wondered if the river would be running at all by the time we reached Thaisan. Walking up we saw more examples of deforestation. Houses and settlements had no trees near them for a hundred metres. Yet away from these settlements the whole area was thick with trees. It was clear the whole area was completely forested before human activity stripped large amounts of the vegetation. But with no other nearby resources, and the wood being so convenient, free and easily accessible it was clear why it had been used, and ultimately would continue being used until some other cheap, accessible, transportable fuel source came about, which was frankly pretty unlikely, at least in the near future.

The trail was very busy. Continuing to climb steeply and unrelentingly up, we passed several farmers and villagers on their way to Jatra from another village. One of them, returning from Thaisan said that were was a lot of snow. Shit, I think, scrambling upwards. As I climb a particularly awful set of stairs cut into the rock, a boy of no more than 8 scampers past. That was how porters were able to carry such heavy loads. They started young. Having not seen any schools in a while, and certainly, not for higher secondary, it's easy to see how education becomes a secondary priority to a family's primary and more urgent needs, often looking after cattle and the farm. Getting out of Darchula appeared to be very difficult indeed.

Later I passed a young couple from Jatra, who were walking it seemed, to get the privacy needed by a young couple, but so hard to find when you're living at home. The man, barely 20, and the girl even younger, were dressed to the hilt. Him in an incredibly shiny silver suit jacket and jeans, her in a spotless sari. It seemed someone hadn't told them that you couldn't go hiking, or even walking, without spending an inordinate amount of money on branded and often garish outdoor gear. As they passed me and climbed I noticed they hadn't broken a sweat, and yet again the girl was in chappals. Once more I looked down at my boots and cursed. Whatsmore, in the fifteen minutes of solitude before they had arrived I had been getting lost in my fantasy. I was trekking alone, the porters and guides never counted in mountaineering memoirs after all, in the furthermost western district of Nepal, in the remotest conservation area in the country. I'd be soon sleeping in tents, camping, drinking snow, living in solitude in an area too harsh for anyone else to live or let alone settle in and generally living a hiking fantasy in the Himalayas. The snow and cold had forced all of the other inhabitants back lower down the valley, but not me. But that was all it was, a fantasy. The trail I romanticised was for a young boy, his path to school, an elderly women's road to the doctors, the grandfathers walk for cigarettes. We all walked the same path to the same destinations yet our journeys could not have been more different.

I reflected, in between difficultly grasped breaths, on the scope of mountaineering books, or at least books on mountains which overwhelming appeared to be written by westerners. They all tended to be of a similar ilk. A lone brave western man, going alone against all the odds in a hostile country or environment and returning with heroic tales to tell. Even better, if they had received a small, but a visible injury on the way, which served as a conversation starter, jumping off point and generally would dominate this person's sense of existence. You only had to walk into a bookshop, particularly in Thamel, to find shelves and shelves of books on mountaineering, from people who are tourists in the mountains. The cover would often have a picture of a bearded western man, usually in a garish walking jacket, with a zany title such as 'I survived Everest, but only just!' These books I felt were all the same but more importantly, were written by the wrong people. The landscape, country and people were only ever merely a backdrop, and as a result, it didn't really matter whether the brave mountaineers was in the Solukhumbu, Patagonia or even the Pennines. The country only served as an indication of how exotic and remote the place was, the heroism was the story, and everything else was just bonus filler. Occasionally, a Nepali would get a mention, but predominately along the lines of 'my Sherpa and I'…or 'Tshering brought me some tea'. It was much easier to write someone out of a story or ignore them all together if you couldn't converse in a shared language. Often in these cases how well someone spoke English was a quick and easy measure of someone's intelligence, regardless of whether it was their fourth or fifth language spoken.

The thing that struck me was the fact these books were effectively written by tourists who didn't live in the area, who had no real connection apart from perhaps spending one month a year there. I wanted a book about the mountains written by someone who grew up there. I didn't necessarily want to hear about the arduous trek from Lukla to Everest Base Camp, yet again, undertaken by a brave courageous trekker, I wanted to read about people for whom that same journey was a daily undertaking just to go to school or the market. I wanted to read about the people who, for them, the mountains are their home, not people who had made the mountain their home. What's more, there was too much romanticism, I wanted some ground truths. I wanted to hear about the difficulties that occurred when living and ultimately staying in the mountains entailed. Why did we so often defer to a westerner when talking about mountain livelihoods? I questioned my own ability to discern properly and realised I too was missing a lot in my own observations. While I might be able to compare the Himalayas to other places in Nepal or compare it with the Alps or the Rockies, my observations where no more than uninformed insights of a slightly knowledgeable trekker. I didn't even speak Khas, so what could I ever ultimately learn? If I reflected, I was from Darchula writing this book, I could have a wealth of more insights, local histories to reflect on. A book from a porter or guide would be fascinating, not just for the difference in perspective but the things they will have seen change over twenty to thirty years. But I was not a guide or a porter, nor was I from Darchula so I was never going to be able to write the book I wanted to read. I too was just a tourist in the mountains. Feeling rather hypocritical I carried on scribbling in my notebook.

As I climbed, I thought back to the many people that I had spoken to on the trip, who enthusiastically encouraged me to recommend

ANCA, to show my pictures back in Kathmandu and to promote the area. They are desperate for the rewards of tourism and envious of the wealth of the Solukhumbu. What's more many of the tourists that did come to Darchula were heading to Api, the highest peak in Western Nepal. What this meant though was the trips were often arranged over the counter in London, Berlin or New York and the trips were self-sufficient. They would be picked up by a jeep at Dhanghadi airport and whisked straight away by jeep to the trailhead, with all the tents, supplies and food they would need ready to be loaded up on porters. While this was a great hassle free expedition for those short on time but not money, it was debatable what benefit that it had to the locals. The permit fees all went to Kathmandu. Food, lodging and porters were the only things left that were needed from Darchula, and these big fully supported trips avoided two out of those three things.

We had been walking for almost two hours when out of the corner of my eye, I saw a wild fox. It was walking high up to my left and was scarcely visible in the bushes. Then half an hour later I saw another fox walking behind some cattle. When the heat from the climb got too much, I drank from the river and doused my face in its cold water. The freezing cold glacial water would make me shiver all over. Eagles flew ahead and dove down the valley as we finally came out of the trees. Looking to my left, high above I could see what looked to be the summit of a pass.

It was almost another hour's climb before I reached the top of the pass. When I did a whole vista came into view. A bell, Shiva trident and the remains of a small and old almost collapsed mandir marked the pass. It was around 3800 metres above sea level. I gazed upon what must have been a one hundred and eighty-degree panorama, an eclectic mix of snow, rock and exposed peaks. They were all in India, the Uttarakhand Himalayas, and I could almost see into Nanda Devi National Park. Below me, forests and grassland stretched out before me, and a few kilometres ahead and a couple of hundred metres below us was Thaisan. The view was stunning and not for the first time I realised the futility at attempting to describe it with mere words. Snow covered the ground and crunched beneath my feet as I sat at the top, breathing heavily and waited for the others to arrive. Looking down back to Jatra the view was all hills, behind me now was all Himalayas. Last year I had travelled to Sikkim and stared past Kanchenjunga into Nepal. This time I was in Nepal staring into India. From our vantage point, you couldn't see the Mahakali itself, but you could make out the gorge that it had carved for itself. As international borders go it was pretty stunning. I thought again about the old Gorkha Empire stretching around me, now the empire's glory is confined to the annals of history books.

After twenty or so minutes Narayan and Ramji came into view, Ramji had paused just below the summit to smoke. As hard as the five-hour climb was for me, I didn't have thirty kilos on my back, nor was I on the second day of a fast. After we had stopped, Ramji smoked two more victory cigarettes, his fast it appeared wasn't restricting his vice, and after having taken the customary photographs we headed down. But the new valley we now climbed down into was thick with snow. Stumbling down the snow-covered trail we headed to Thaisan, which was tough going. The sections in the sun had frozen, melted, and refrozen into ice. As a result here you could walk onto the snow, yet in the shade, you just fell through. Or seemingly I did, once again I blamed my overly heavy boots. The next day I had planned to go Bhramhadaha, a lake apparently both visited and blessed by Lord Brahma, and to Siddhatopi a holy mountaintop, both were situated higher than Thaisan. As a result, we had planned to camp just down from the pass and above Thaisan, to minimize the following days climbing. Yet when we arrived at the camping area, it was still under two feet of snow and all the rivers had frozen. We had, not for the first time it would later emerge, a water issue. There was no running mountain stream from which we could collect water. Instead, a frozen brook stood painfully empty. There was, Narayan said, a tap

Photo 7: Looking down to the Thaisan Plateau

down in Thaisan so it would be much easier if we headed down to the plateau and camped there with access to fresh water. Looking around slightly perplexed at all the snow around, I didn't figure there to be a water issue, but I could see Thaisan below and there didn't appear to be much snow. Assenting, more to not camp deep in snow, I agreed and we headed down. The trail snaked its way through snow filled forests and with the pine trees in the foreground and Himalayas in the background made for a truly alluring view. Walking, especially with all the climbing for the day done, was an incredibly relaxing way to wind down. We passed to our left a small glacial lake with a green and blue hue. I asked Narayan what it was called, Thaisan Tal he replied disinterestedly. I was never sure whether that was its actual name. I had started to distrust some of the names Narayan gave places, particularly after when the day before I had asked him the name of another small lake, he'd merely replied "sano tal."

After an hour or so down from the peak of the pass we reached Thaisan. It was a large grassland plateau, currently uninhabited. I could see why the entire ground was frozen with patchy snow. We passed farms, terraces and even saw some wild horses up ahead. There were numerous stone huts nearby. Arriving in one, I dumped my bags before pitching my tent in front of the Himalayas while Narayan and Navinder started cooking. Ramji went off looking for this elusive water source. Half an hour later after struggling to place my pegs in the frozen ground, I was relaxing and feeling very smug and content. I had owned this tent for several years and been lucky to camp in some truly remarkable places, but this was something else. In front of me, the terraces fell away into the valley floor and you could see the riverbank at the bottom. Then climbing up from the riverbank was the Himalayan foothills before they gave way to the Himalayas themselves. This must have been a visible altitude change of several thousand metres. Sitting inside my tent, the terraces below were out of view. All I could see from the open flap of my tent door where the lofty peaks of the Himalayas. Their white tips were slowly turning crimson in the hue of the early afternoon sun.

The others were staying in an empty hut, apparently built by the government a few years ago, and had stretched out and made a fire. However, the much-discussed tap had either frozen or the tank was empty. What then followed was the nearest thing on the whole trip that could be accounted to an argument or disagreement.

'So Max we are having water issues' Narayan started off.

'Yeah it's not ideal, but we have lots of snow'

'We do, but the porters going to go and collect water from the lake'

'Which lake?' I replied feeling confused, had I missed another lake on the way down. Surely he didn't mean the algae green glacial lake?

'The glacial lake', Narayan replied proving my fears wrong.

'But that's filthy' I protested

'No, no, no, its glacial water its fine. It's direct from the mountains. There's no problem'.

'Can we not just melt snow?' I asked, not really fancying my luck with the alternative

'But it takes too long'

'Longer than walking a 40 minute round trip for a few litres a time?'

In the end, we comprised and I went off to collect snow, which wasn't too hard with it being pilled around the hut, while Ramji and Narvinder went off to fill their pots with dirty water.

Later when they returned, the water looked even worse in the filthy plastic jars. The kind of jar I used to store black-market petrol. I wasn't alone in using that jar for petrol I thought, looking at the filthy plastic container, and getting a heady scent when I sniffed the contents of the jar

After another heated discussion, the green glacial water, in the end, was used to soak the rajma and then poured into the pressure cooker and the melted snow would be left for the rice and for drinking.

We sat in the stone hut, after first having swept it off shards of glass from broken bottles of whisky and empty cigarettes packets, torn playing cards and empty packets of chewing tobacco. A common sight in these places. With two wooden fires blazing it was warm inside the hut, but with no chimney or windows open it soon became incredibly smoky. After an hour or so of warming up, I had to step outside to give my streaming eyes and raw chest a break.

When I stepped outside, by the sun was setting over the Himalayas, lending them a pink aurora behind them which reflected in the snow resting on their peaks. I called Narayan over and we sat and stared into India. I felt at that moment so happy I burst out laughing, much to the bemusement and perplexment of Narayan, and it had to be said, myself.

After the sun had set we returned to the hut. Once the rajma and rice had cooked we sat there in silence before unceremoniously diving into the food with our hands. I was tired and hungry, but nothing compared to Ramji who, for his first meal in 2 days ate and ate. After several plates of rice, he sat back burped, then farted before lighting a beedi and sat there with what almost passed for a look of contentment on his face.

An hour later I was interrupted from my thoughts by a deep rumble and the sound of falling earth. I shot up immediately thinking it was from an earthquake and that I'd heard a resulting landslide. I was luckily only half right, it was an avalanche high up in the mountains, and we were close enough to hear it and almost feel the rumble of snow and earth tumbling down at an immense speed reverberating and pulsating through the ground we sat on. Thank god it wasn't an earthquake I thought. I laughed nervously attempting to pass off any fear, but truth be told I was still scared of another earthquake, particularly all the way out here with no communication.

I was in Nepal during the Gorkha earthquakes of 2015, and I had studied both the geological phenomena of earthquakes and how to manage them. A significant proportion of my time in Tribhuvan University was spent going to a plethora of conferences, debates and presentations regarding the earthquake so earthquakes were always in the back of my mind. I knew, or at least had heard by a number of experts, only some of whom were self-proclaimed, that the Far-West was long overdue its own major earthquake. As I looked around I tried to work out just how damaging it would be. Lots of the deaths in the Gorkha earthquakes of 2015 were preventable and ultimately due to the poor design and construction of houses, some of which were several stories too high. It was a much-repeated mantra in Kathmandu, that it was in fact buildings, not earthquakes which killed people. Here, without the skyscrapers or big poorly planned buildings, it was clear that that threat at least did not exist. A lack of open safe spaces in Kathmandu and in other built-up areas also led to the high casualty list, again in Darchula a lack of open space was not an issue. Yet I thought, the major issue here would be transported and dealing with the sheer remoteness of the place. With only one road into Khalanga, an earthquake-induced landslide could easily block access to the area, already poorly served by medical treatment facilities. In many ways, people living here were more resilient and prepared than others in the country certainly compared to the capital, purely as they had to be due to their remoteness, yet there was a real dearth of proper medical facilities and supplies which could easily manifest from a huge issue into a disaster. Getting humanitarian aid out here would be a serious challenge, even chartering a helicopter to the hospitals of Kathmandu was more expensive. It is around $2,000 for a one-way helicopter trip from the central Himalayas, i.e. Annapurna and Everest, yet for Darchula and nearby districts, I had heard quotes of much nearer to $12,000. Travelling around the far-west was already difficult enough without an onslaught of tremors and landslides. What's more, while the houses were not dangerously high they were old and many rather decrepit. I would lie awake at night, more than once, with the thought of a tremor dislodging the seemingly haphazardly laid dry stone walling of some huts we would stay in, and be unable to sleep due to visions of being buried under a pile of slate. Nepal had a number of issues to deal with, lying in the most seismically active region in the world was not an extra challenge anyone relished with enthusiasm.

Later sitting by the fire a heated conversation broke out, Ramji, was complaining about the marriage of his daughter and the high price of the dowry. He was looking at having to spend around 5 lakh on his daughter's wedding, I wondered where he'd get the money from. But the worst of it, as he went on, was the fact his daughter was marrying a Thapa Magar, not a Bahun like himself. Everyone nodded, this was a serious matter indeed. I sat back, full and tired and tried to listen to as much as I could understand. Half an hour later, too tired to feign comprehension anymore I left the hut and collapsed in my tent.

I woke with a shiver at 3, in the middle of the night it was freezing. I was wearing all my clothes, all my jackets and was in a sleeping bag. Yet it was still bitterly cold, and I couldn't stop shivering. I'd spent cold nights in a tent before and found nothing worse. The rain was one thing, but there was nothing you could do about the cold, certainly not sleep through it. As I curled up into the foetal position shivering and waiting till dawn I just hoped that my stomach would hold until morning. As cold as it was in my tent, the idea of going to the toilet outside and have body parts exposed to the icy climate at that time of the morning seemed all too inhumane. I hoped the glacier water wouldn't violently resurface before the sun rose.

The next morning once I left my tent, I realised the source of my discomfort. It had snowed last night and there was a thick layer of frost on the outside of my tent as well as a foot of snow on the ground. Cold, tired and in a frankly foul mood I went into the hut. Inside it was the very picture of comfort and fraternity with all three men curled up around the fire. What's more, it was very warm inside. I sat next to the dying embers of last night's fire and tried to warm my bones while drinking some barely deforested snow water. I cursed my tent and wish I'd spent the night inside around a fire, as opposed to outside alone shivering in a thinly layered tent. The romanticism of staying in a tent had provided too alluring and I had paid the price.

At around seven, after a scarcely filling breakfast of biscuits and cold water, Ramji and I set off up to Bramhadaha and Sidhatopi, while Narayan would pack up and Navinder would head back down to Jatra. We had planned to spend two nights in Thaisan but with no water and the snow, we decided to head down to Sina that night, as it was around 1000 metres below Thaisan and if nothing else it would be warmer than last night and at the very least there would be less snow.

We climbed up the same path we had descended yesterday, only today it had an even thicker covering of snow. Cold, tired and not having had a cup of tea, let alone coffee, I struggled on. With increasing familiarity, I repeatedly fell almost waist deep in snow, again my boots falling through the areas that Ramji could almost skip over with him wearing what looked suspiciously like tennis

Photo 8: Camping in Thaisan

shoes. Today with no bags to carry, and finally having broken his fast, he set a blistering pace. I did my best to keep up, luckily his prevalence for smoking offered me some respite. With me catching up to him, inevitably as soon he took the last drag of a cigarette before setting off again, we at least made good time. After an hour we had climbed several hundred metres and had passed last nights proposed camping spot, abandoned due to lack of water. I was in two minds, one regretting having left the higher camp yesterday for non-existent water only to drag myself back up the next day, and another, slightly more rational, looking around the waist-high snow and being glad we had not spent a night up here. If it had been cold in Thaisan it may well have been unbearable here.

After two hours climb, we reached Bramhadha, a small lake nestled in a little depression, surrounded by pristine fresh snow. To the left of the lake you could see the start of the Api Himal range, the

Photo 9: Looking down from Siddhatopi to the lower Nepali hills

one time on the trip I would actually see the snow-covered peaks of the Nepali Himalayas, the rest of the trip having stared into the Indian Himalayas. From here standing higher than the previous day's, we were afforded a fantastic vantage point, surrounded by mountains on three sides, and with the snow-covered forests of the hills behind me. Catching my breath I stared at the lake. It had apparently been visited by Lord Brahma, the creator, who'd blessed it before leaving again. Although to me it looked like it hadn't been visited by anyone for a while. Ramji lit up another foul cigarette, I was amazed just how awful it smelt and how it was able to mask the otherwise fresh mountain air. It smelt like a mixture of cheap plastic and cow dung. When I found out the price of a packet, it wouldn't have surprised me if I was right.

Later after walking past Siddhatopi, we headed back down to Thaisan. Walking in snow through the Himalayas sounds incredibly

Photo 10: Wild horses in the snow

romantic, but the reality is less so. It was exhausting and when it got muddy there was a horrible brown slush all over the trail. Snow I realised, not for the first time, was much nicer to look at than to be in.

Arriving back at the campsite everything was packed up, and Narayan and Navinder were lazing in the sun. Considering just how cold it had been only three hours ago it was now positively warm, almost sunbathing weather. I laid down in the sun for a few minutes. After I few minutes some movement caught my eye, I looked over to the right and three wild horses came into view. Two were a chestnut brown and the other an off eggshell white. They grazed and whinnied maybe 15 metres in front of me. I had never seen wild horses before this trip and these were truly elegant. One approached a fence, stared at it contemplatively for a few seconds before jumping over it and galloping off. Its friends, either startled by the noise or just caught up in the excitement, followed the horse and they had soon trotted out of sight.

I must have drifted off to sleep in the sun and woke with a start a few minutes later. I went to pay Navinder so he could head back to Jatra and we could walk down to Sina.

Sina

From here we would depart our small camp on the Thaisan plateau and journey on towards Sina. At this point, we had no water, and with the midday sun soon to rise, that wasn't the greatest position to be in. I asked Narayan whether we should melt some snow but he assured me there was no need as only several minutes down the hill there was a plentiful selection of streams and rivers from which we could drink from. Nodding my head in assent we set off down to Sina almost a thousand metres below. Heading down we saw more evidence of farming and crops, Narayan told me in mid-march farmers would return from their houses lower down the valley to cultivate the area. The area is well known in the region for grazing and crop cultivation and is frankly a beautiful if the slightly inconvenient place for growing vegetables. Walking down the valley there was no real trail so we picked our way down terraces laden with snow-covered rocks and roots. It was noticeably warmer heading down and we soon started to shed our layers. Desperate by this stage for a drink we passed a river, but it was frozen further upstream and there was no water trickling down. This would become an all too common phenomenon over the next few hours.

The view was historic, and with old stone huts on the terraces, it looked unchanged for centuries. It was hard to imagine who may have walked here hundreds of years ago. These now peaceful, quiet pastures were once home to bustling traders, farmers and all in between. A band of Limi traders perhaps, on their way heading back to Tibet. A Rajput breathing easily having put a safe distance between himself and Mughal aggressors. Or maybe a Khas solider returning from Jumla. Now it was quiet. It felt, with no-one around, forgotten. Today there was no one here walking except us. And yet what a historic place this was.

The famed Kingdom of Gorkha would, in fact, find its roots in the Khas Empire. After the fall of the Khas empire in the 15th century, many chiefs and soldiers moved east seizing dominions, some of these conquerors moved to Gorkha. What would eventually become the home of Prithvi Narayan Shah and the seat of the Gurkha Kingdom

Today vestiges of former glory are missing. The Khas Kingdom was soon forgotten, except inside notes about the history of the Gorkhas. A few months later when re-reading 'A voyage to Nepal', I stumbled on the following extracts. In his account of a journey to Nepal made in 1885, the French social psychologist and polymath, Gustave Le Bon,

"Before becoming masters of the valley of Nepal, the Gurkhas were one of the warrior tribes that dwelt in Nepal. They claim descent from the Rajput's who long ago migrated to the country, feeling the Muslim conquest".

Another slightly backhanded mention of the Khas is offered again when he traces the history of the word Gurkha, which according to Le Bon, "does not at all determine a definite race. It is used in Nepal to designate the descent of any class or origin who at the end of the last century left the Nepalese province of Gurkha to exert the power on the rest of Nepal. They form, according to their origin, different castes. The highest one, the Kshatriya, descents from an alliance between Rajput's and women of a primitive tribe called the Khas".

The history in Nepal's hills runs deep yet its scars are not as obvious as those of the boulders fallen from landslides. There is little left here to remain witness to the skirmishes, fights, expansions and shrinkages of the old Nepalese old kingdoms.

Two hours after leaving Thaisan I am now completely parched. I hadn't drunk a lot of water yesterday due to my concerns that it was dirty and now I was in desperate need of a drink. We had come a long way through small forests and terraces, but not past a water source. The cold of the Himalayas was now long gone as we had quickly dropped altitude. The sun was out in force and I started to feel light headed. With nothing productive to do, I decided to feel bitter and angry about everything. I cursed Narayan for not bottling more water, I cursed Ramji for waking me up early every morning with his desire to smoke near me, I cursed my friend in the police for saying I wouldn't have an issue with Khas. I was in a fantastically foul mood while walking through the forest that led us to Sina, I couldn't see the wood for the trees.

We passed yet another stream that too, again mockingly it was empty of any water. However less than five minutes later though, I turned a corner to see a little bubbling beck and crystal clear water. It was heaven. I bent down to my knees and drank heartily from the river, the water was so cold that it affected my teeth but I didn't care. I stayed on my knees until I had drunk half a litre from my cupped hands and then proceeded to wash my face and body from yesterday's smoke and soot. I leant back, burped and felt content but also

Photo 11: Standing in front of the Api Himal

incredibly stupid. As my anger disappeared with my thirst I took a look around at exactly where I was, what a place to be and what a place to walk. How stupid that sheer thirst had put me in such a foul mood, I was glad that I had just walked behind and sulked as opposed to actually giving voice to those rash opinions.

Feeling refreshed we headed on to Sina, a small village situated on the lower banks of a valley, sprawled out amongst the terraces and flanked by high rising hills. Directly opposite the town lay a huge landslide, the remains must have been a kilometre wide and several hundred metres high; Narayan told me it happened a few years ago and luckily no-one died. I asked what caused it and he said it was where the locals harvested wood. This led to advanced levels of soil erosion eventually culminating in the degradation of the soil and the resulting landslide. Deforestation had struck again. As we followed winding lanes lined by dry stone walls down through the village we come across a bit of commotion and what looked like a village meeting. There were several elderly men holding themselves up high while talking to a group of elderly women. The women were complaining loudly about something as the men try to reason with them. Ah, I thought, politics. I assumed from the dress, stance and behaviour of these men that they can't be Maoists or UML, they must be Congress. I was right. We had decided to stay in a hut again that night, and not wanting to freeze again in a tent I quickly assented. The hut, however, was opposite the clearing where the impromptu meeting was taking place. I stood and listened, they were talking about the upcoming local elections and the women were discussing their grievances while the men attempted to persuade them things would be better under them, although from the angry faces of the women I suspected they weren't doing a particularly good job. After half an hour or so the meeting wound to an end, mercifully there were no slogans or chanting to follow. A women attached to Congress went around giving everyone a sweet from a big bag. I thought it may take more than a piece of hard candy to win over this crowd as I accepted a sweet myself. Election fever had gripped the town and it was nice to come down from the hills into a strong debate.

That evening we spent holed up in our hut. The political debate, with only twenty people there it could hardly be called a rally, ended up turning into, as these things often do in the countryside to a village drinking session. Almost forty men had taken the place of the politicians, except they held glasses of rakhsi as opposed to clipboards. At about 4 pm, I noted there were 3 grown men unable to stand. I had no idea how they would manage the one hour walk back, in the oncoming darkness to their houses. The men were naturally less concerned about their travel plans than I was. Once the Congress men had left, locals continued to congregate, drink and swap stories about politicians. A few hours after the drinking had started and I had broken conversation with several incredibly drunk farmers, I decided on the face of it, as voices rose along with the drink, that maybe hiding in my hut with a drink might be a more fortuitous, and certainly easier use of my time.

The hut we were staying in had two storeys, the lower one served as a tea and rakshi shop, whilst I was sitting directly above that on the beams of the second floor, a room used for storage. Being only several feet above the congregation I could not only hear their conservation, which was managing to quickly decay into a drunken debacle but I could also hear the crackle of the fire and the smell of their cigarettes. It had been a long day, I leant back against the wall and closed my eyes.

Dinner, rice and the now daily rajma, came along soon enough. A filling meal, but I had to admit three people sharing a close space for several days eating beans and pulses had meant a lot of flatulence, particularly from Ramji. It was shortly after dinner when Ramji was making sure to digest his food with as much noise as possible that I wished for the first time he would start smoking those god-awful cigarettes and mask one bad smell with one just slightly more tolerable.

Following dinner, Narayan and I shared a bottle of whisky in what had now become a nightly ritual. We were sipping our drinks and Narayan was discussing local politics when all of a sudden the door at the end of the room burst open and in walked 6 men, all in similar states of inebriation. The biggest man, who seemed to be the de-facto leader walked over to us, which didn't take long as the room was hardly big, and attempted to introduce himself. He was huge, a big stocky man with tikka smeared roughly on his forehead and pupils that screamed of drink. Apparently, I found out later, they had heard a foreigner was in their village and they had wanted to welcome me. Except at that moment, it didn't feel like a welcoming party. There was me, Narayan and Ramji surrounded 6 fully grown men drunk beyond belief. We were pinned against the corner, while so far the mood was amicable, I'd been in these situations before and knew just how fast things could deteriorate and turn downhill. The leader introduced himself or at least tried to in broken English.

'*You, country which from?*' He slurred at me.

'*England*', I replied.

Following which he uttered several completely unintelligible sentences which for the life of me I couldn't follow. They certainly weren't in English, but nor were they not in English. One sentence he repeated several times, and I simply wasn't able to answer. I told him I didn't understand, he didn't seem particularly happy at this news. It must have been embarrassing for him, acting as the leader of his friends as he spoke English, only not to be understood by a westerner. This, I thought, must be a similar experience to a Khas speaker trying to understand me. His friends started then asking questions in Khas, directed to Narayan. Where was I from, where was I going, did I have any cigarettes, did I have any booze? I feigned ignorance and didn't reply, and tried to focus all of my attention on a particularly interesting stain on the floor.

After five minutes, which seemed significantly longer, they had finished all their own cigarettes, and booze. With no rakshi forthcoming from us, I had hidden the bottle behind me when they entered, they eventually got bored of talking amongst themselves and left to get some more booze. As soon as the last man had clambered, almost falling, out of the door Ramji scarpered over to the door, locked and bolted it.

Narayan turned to me '*Do you know who that man was?*' he asked with a smirk.

'*Not a clue*' I replied.

'*He was the local English teacher, the headmaster of the school in Sina*' Narayan giggled, and it wasn't long before I joined in. That explained a lot. It also explained his anger at not being understood. It must have been embarrassing for him not being understood, or at least it would have been had he not been so drunk. I was glad they'd left, people this drunk were quick to anger and out here that often lead to violence. Not wanting to blend in with the people hanging around Khalanga at night with various facial scars I looked at the locked door, smiled and drew out a second bottle of whisky and poured myself and Narayan another drink.

Huti

Waking early I left the hut to stretch my legs. Evidence of last night's debauchery was not hard to find. A mountain of cigarettes butts and broken glass from a multitude of bottles marked the door to the tea shop. Today we would leave Sina and head to Huti, staying there for a final night before heading back to Khalanga.

Over the last few days, I had noticed Ramji riffling through my big holdall bag. He kept his own small bag inside mine, with his spare shirt and chappals. I'd thought he'd just been re-arranging the bag to make the load easier to bear. Apart from books, food and clothes, there was nothing of any value inside the bag and I wrote off any ill feeling as just his curiosity over my possessions and what he was carrying. Yet this morning, before we set off, I returned from outside to the room to find him munching happily away on some of my granola bars. I looked over, Narayan was eating one too.

'*You want one?*' he offered graciously in between bites.

From then on, I would regularly see Ramji and Narayan tucking into my food, which wasn't a real issue. But I had packed food enough for one person for a week, not for three. As this went on my supplies of food began to dwindle rapidly.

Photo 12: Looking into Uttarakhand

On the trail again we quickly left Sina behind. After a while the Mahakali came back into view, it wouldn't leave my sight again until I left Khalanga. We walked down a valley divided by the Mahakali and yet again stared into India. As the Mahakali came back into view, we came to a police post. From the post, the police can see right down and along the Mahakali and therefore the border. A great vantage spot but it can't rival that of the now almost constant humming of Indian helicopters monitoring the border and flying out supplies to its equally remote border police force. The two policemen stationed at the post, both from Dadeldhura were clearly bored to tears. They took my passport check as an excuse for a break and we went off for tea and chowmein. As we have tea and they talk about the local elections, just how bored they must be hits home. There is nothing to do here, this trail is no real thoroughfare nor are any other trekkers coming through. The extent of their boredom is made clear when one of the policeman, Shiva, announced he needs to go to the police station in Sunsera to take over a small log. I try not to laugh at this terrible invention of an excuse to bunk off and asked him to join us, which he was clearly angling for all along. As we walk side by side, Shiva, Narayan and I, Shiva takes the opportunity to practise his English. We engaged in small talk for the hour or so it takes to reach Sunsera, where he walked up the hill to the police station and deposits his log. Right next to, I couldn't help but notice, a large pile of other much larger logs.

I had seen on this trip, numerous examples of deforestation and spent numerous nights in small stone huts huddled around a fire for hours. The next day my throat and eyes would inevitably be raw, sore and red from all the smoke. The deforestation was a major issue, as was the use of open fires for heating and cooking. It had provoked much worry and condemnation from NGOs in Kathmandu, often promoting new and improved methods of heating or cooking. Yet these were often highly unsuitable for the local environment or capacity. Out here I thought, what choice do you have? If you're faced with using the wood that is freely available outside your house or buying an expensive gas stove and then having to hire a porter for several days to bring new gas canister to your house, it wasn't a difficult choice to make. How many people particularly in Kathmandu, I wondered, so self-righteous in their angst, would not adopt exactly the same habits instinctively if they lived here?

After a few hours, we passed through the next village, where we planned to stay for lunch. There's a small hut we passed and when we did, I heard shouting inside that was almost incoherent and didn't sound like either Nepali or Khas. Narayan told me we were going to stop here for lunch, leaving me completely confused. All of the shouting and commotion is emerging from one room, I peered inside. There was an old Nepali man, covered in prayer beads, with thick deep golden earrings and a topi, shouting while throwing rice all over the room. In front of him were three people, an old man, a young boy who I assume to be his son and another old man. They all had rice and vermilion not just smeared on their forehead, but all over their faces, I could see spare grains of rice nestled on their shoulders and in their hair. This must be a shaman. Withdrawing I asked Narayan and he confirmed my suspicions. We sat outside and listened for a few minutes until the ceremony was over.

A few minutes later with the ceremony over, everyone left the room and a small girl entered the room and started sweeping up the rice from the floor before putting it back into a container, complete with added dust. The shaman came out, his eyes I noticed were incredibly vivid and clear. He namaskered me, I returned it. Then, before I could protest he smeared rice on my head in a crude form of Tikka. Next, bizarrely he asked Narayan how many people needed food before reaching under the bench outside and bringing out 6 onions and a knife and started to chop them. I had met Shamans before, but I'd never had one make my lunch. I sat and watched him chop vegetables while the rice on my forehead slowly dropped off, grain by grain. I turned my attention to the other people, the old man and his son sat on a bench next to him while the other old man walked off. The man with his son I notice was fiddling with a beedi. I see him empty it out, pull out a small ball of hash from his shirt pocket, make a mixture and re-roll his beedi. He lights it with a flick of his match and contently pulls heavily on his small improvised joint. After choking down his crude joint, he immediately starts to make another and begins talking. His accent is thick and I can't make out what he's saying. For the next hour, as the Shaman chops vegetables and starts to cook, this man continually rolls and smokes joints. As he does he becomes a lot more animated and it was clear by the tone or his voice, facial and physical gestures he's talking about something serious. Some 6 joints later, as our food arrives he eats with one hand, still smoking with the other. We eat rice and rajma again, but this time with ghee. After mopping up the rest of the rajma with my hand I leant back, full and content. After eating the man tapped his son on the shoulder, stood up, slightly unsteadily and they walked off.

I ask Narayan what he was talking about. *'Ah Max, that man is having a very bad time. His oldest son died a few weeks ago, and all he has left is that boy. But the boy doesn't speak and hasn't eaten for days. So he came to the Shaman to see what he could do.'* Looking back I realised the boy hadn't said a word nor made a sound. The old man's desperate pulling on his joint adopted a new, much darker significance. While the puja hadn't restored the boy's voice, the boy had eaten. A small victory I thought wryly.

We followed the path, which soon became a road almost wide enough to accommodate a vehicle, a motor road Narayan says. Although with the number of boulders littering the path, not even a motorbike could ride this, let alone a car. The road has been crudely constructed and was supported by half filed crates of rocks.

Here with all the climbing over and the road relatively flat, we made good time and it wasn't long before we arrived in Huti, a small settlement with a few government outposts and shops. We found a place to eat dinner and rest, the owner as it turns out is a retired Indian police inspector. It couldn't have been later than 2 pm and knowing we only had 3 or 4 hours of walking on flat ground the next day before we would reach Khalanga. It was time for celebration. I spoke to Narayan and we decided to go have a beer.

We headed up out of Huti, to find a terrace to sit and relax. A few kilometres out of town we found a suitable place to sit. Directly in front of me, once again was Uttarakhand and below me and the terraces were the Mahakali, which was starting to gain both volume and speed.

I opened our beers and passed one to Narayan. It seemed a good place to sit and reflect on our journey. Short but remarkable, difficult and rewarding in equal measures. As I looked for one of the last times at the tri-colour of the Indian flag on the other side of the river I was disturbed from my tranquillity by a large painful feeling in my shoulder and a thud to my right. I looked and saw a rock by my side, the rock was at least the size of a small plant pot. Another one quickly landed beside it. The realisation that someone was throwing rocks at us quickly dawned upon is. Next, I heard the shouting of an older man. I was immediately alert, the voice has the tone of authority and instantly thought police, although I wasn't not sure why. Narayan put down his beer, stood up and was immediately involved in a confrontation. As I rubbed my shoulder, now very sore, I heard him protest that he was with a tourist, we were here to relax and were doing nothing wrong. This was met with a volley of sound from the old man, who continued to shout as, mercifully, he started to walk away. Narayan sat back down again, picked up his beer and continued drinking as if nothing had happened and with no explanation. Clearly, my expression must have been pretty worried as he laughs and slaps me on the back.

'Don't worry Max, he was just an old farmer!'

'A farmer? What was he mad about?'

'Ah you see this is his field', Narayan said pointing to the area we were sitting on, *'and he has lots of problems with small kids coming and shitting on his land. He said he saw your feet sticking up of the terrace and thought you were a kid taking a shit so he threw a stone.'* I looked at Narayan slightly incredulously and we burst out laughing. Not wanting to get hit by any more rocks we walk back down to Huti while I wonder about modern parenting methods in the far-west.

I sat down in Huti outside our lodge and watched the world go by. The primary traffic of the road was made up of chickens, goats and dogs. I watched as the policeman's dog stared off the attention of another smaller dog. They ended up chasing each other running down the road barking. As I sat down outside the house and drank my tea, I watched about 8 children come out of a nearby house and run around. Except on closer inspection, only about 4 were playing and they are all boys. The girls who must be as young as 6 were pounding millet, moving cattle, cleaning up and generally learning how to run the house. Many of these children would probably never go to school and certainly not high school. The clothes that most children were wearing were significantly older than you see in other parts of Nepal. It's a tough life here, with little to no opportunities apart from farming or manual labour. It doesn't take long before India starts to look appealing.

Later as I watched people come and go, I noticed people appeared to be more formal in their way of speaking, more Namaskars to Namastes. When passing people on the trail you would press your palms together, while this is a common ritual all over Nepal, I had not seen it adhered to as strictly. Even if someone's hands were full, they still attempted to at least press their wrists together. I figured due to the area being remote that traditions are less diluted, particularly compared to more metropolitan areas of the country.

Later the sunset and I was still sat there, surrounded by 20 chickens and a cockerel and the same goats. As the hens surrounded a goat he got scared, bleated and tried to run away sending the hens scattering. The policeman's wife came up and fed the dog an old roti and the goat some old rice. I turned around and saw her buffalo emerging from underneath the ground story of their house.

That night around nine pm, I walked into our room. Narayan was rifling through my bag at an alarming speed, with a worried expression on his face.

'What's up?' I asked

'Max', he asked. 'Where is all the food?'

'There should be some in the bag', I replied

'*No, there's none left*', he asked slightly accusingly.

'*Where did it go?*' he continued

To this, I could only meekly reply. '*You ate it all*'. With Khalanga only a few kilometres away from this luckily would not pose a problem. I resolved next time to take more food.

Khalanga

The next day we left Huti early, planning on having lunch back in Khalanga Bazaar. With our minds already thinking the trip was over there was a very leisurely pace to our trip. I knew the hard bit was over, there would be no more real climbing and the cramp in my legs would soon be over. I looked forward to a warm bath, fresh chicken and a cold beer. But I wasn't sure what I wanted more or first.

The sun was already up high and there was little to no clouds at all. As we walked villages began to be more populated, there were more roadside stalls and vehicles had started appearing on the road. Having no worries or stress I allowed my eyes to wander and again they became fixed on the Indian side of the Mahakali. There was something almost unsettling, or something that had gotten under my skin about seeing a country so close, in places I could have thrown a stone into India yet not be allowed in. As I couldn't cross the border in Khalanga I would have had to travel down to Mahendranagar and then travel all the way back up again. Looking across it is not hard to see the material differences between the two countries. The Indian side had roads that were blacktopped and boasted a big government and civil service presence when there was, or at least it felt like it, little to none on the Nepali side apart from the odd small police post. Even with only a short glance, India looked a lot more affluent than the Nepali side. It was.

The road we walked on was dusty and a bit of an eyesore. As we walked I thought back to things that I had read and spoken to many people about the development of other parts of the Himalayas. While many environmental groups, tour operators and trekkers may be disdainful about road construction and infrastructural development, the locals are not. The roads do increase the level of dust, it does spoil an otherwise untouched part of the world, but why should a foreign trekker have a say in the area where they come for only 2 weeks once every few years? I remembered speaking to people in Manang a few years ago about the road around Annapurna, and they were perplexed there would even be a debate. Expectant mothers could now give birth in a hospital. A farmer could send his goods down to the bazaar before they perished. Children in boarding schools didn't have to walk for several days to return home at the end of the term. It seemed so wrong I thought for other people to dictate how other people should live. Did anyone begrudge Switzerland for developing roads, ski-lifts and trains in the hills? That would not even be a tenable point to make. So why then did it work in the Himalayas? Was having someone nice to look at more important than the welfare of the local population? Obviously not.

It was not long before the road swung to the left and then in front of us, several kilometres downstream we saw the outline of Khalanga and the silver wire bridge of the border. We were back, one day earlier than anticipated. Now the road was busy with trucks, keeps as well as tractors. We continued walking.

Just before noon, we arrived back into Khalanga and with our priorities clear we first stopped off for masu bhat. It tasted fantastic after a long break, we hadn't eaten meat since the rabbit in Jatra. I paid Ramji off and he walked over to my hotel with my bags, before starting on his return to Dailekh. I went to pay Narayan before realising he had drunk, and Ramji had smoked, considerably more than I had budgeted for so I went to the ATM, which naturally wasn't working. Giving Narayan my card he popped over to the Indian side and returned half an hour later with the news that there was no ATM working on that side either. Agreeing to meet tomorrow morning we shook hands and I went off in search of a barber, cold booze and a hot shower. I made a booking on a bus to Dhangadi for the next day and stumbled into my hotel room. I manage to stay awake long enough to shower with a bucket of warm water and down a beer before falling asleep fully clothed into a deep slumber.

The next day I woke up and walked back into the bazaar. I meet Narayan again by the ATM. Today as well on both sides of the border the machines aren't working. He gives me the name of a cousin he has in Kathmandu and I agree to give him the money in Kathmandu. With that a warm handshake, a hug and promises to meet up in Kathmandu, we departed and I went to wait for my bus back down to the plains.

The Beyul of
the Rolwaling Valley

Simigaon

The names of Everest, Annapurna, and Kanchenjunga are synonymous with mountaineering in Nepal. Yet the Rolwaling valley never gained the same prominence of its neighbours, tucked in-between Langtang and the Solukhumbu, and on the face of it at least appeared almost forgotten.

I had long heard Rolwaling described as a forgotten or hidden valley, indeed in Gabriele Tautscher's Himalayan Mountain Cults, the first reference to Rolwaling is as one of the *"hidden valleys of Rolwaling, Lapchi and Shubar in the upper reaches of the Tama Kosi valley"*. The valley is home to numerous Sherpa villages first populated by travellers from the Solukhumbu between two and four hundred years ago. The valley differs from most in Nepal with its east to west orientation; this provides a much easier climate for animals to wander. As a result, the valley is home to a large variety of animals including bears, jackals and most notably the snow leopard, and according to some the Yeti. Approximately 300 plant species are able to call the valley home. A study of the valleys spiritual and religious history finds that the Rolwaling valley has much to boast about. According to Buddhist mythology, Gauri Shanker the 7,134m behemoth that dominates the mountain ranges of the valley is said to be the embodiment of Tashi Tseringma the leader of the Tsher Ring Mched Inga, also known as the Five sisters of long life. My old guidebook informs me that

"According to local legends, in the 8ᵗʰ century, Padmasambhava (Guru Rinpoche) meditated in a small cave in the upper Rolwaling valley. Here he subdued those same infamous five female demons residing on Gauri Shanker that Milarepa is also believed to have battled." Whereas for Hindus the same mountaintop is the home of Lord Shiva and his consort Parvati.

Dolakha's history is of great interest, not only by being worthy of a name drop in the epic Ramayana, the destination where the five Pandava brothers fled to, to avoid persecution. Dolakha has played a vital role in the prosperous Tibetan Trade and its proximity to Tibet has not gone unnoticed. At the height of the Tibetan trade and during the reign of King Yaksa Malla of Bhaktapur 1428-1480, his empire expanded far and wide and went onto include Dolakha, useful for increasing trade and links with Tibet, and his trade benefited immensely from the then fortified city of Dolakaha. Following its rule by the Malla kings, in the 15ᵗʰ and 16ᵗʰ century Dolakha managed to regain its independence for a brief period. Yet its strategic location meant it remained highly coveted and in the 18ᵗʰ century it was swallowed up by the Gorkha kingdom of Prithvi Narayan Shah. In the process of 'Sanskritization', there was an influx of Hindus and more land was given to Hindus to weaken the Tamang grip on the district, seen as a threat to Dolakha's stability as part of the Gorkha Empire. Today it remains an important politically fought over the district, except now its battles are fought with the ballot box and the microphone instead of a khukri.

With geography as interesting as its history I could not stay away. The fact a close friend owned a hotel nearby made the trip more viable. With the aim of exploring the valley and making our way to Tso Rolpa, the largest Glacial Lake in Nepal, my friend Herman and

I met in Charikot. It was mid-February and up in the hills, it was still cold. We had spent nights poured over old maps of Dolakha looking for a potential route. There were rumours of snow on the hills further up. We'd also heard that past Beding, the inhabitants of the next village, Na, were still camped out lower down the mountain. As a result, we made sure we packed enough food for the two of us, and a tent in case we couldn't find any lodges open. We were overloaded but ready. Looking at Gauri Shanker which dominated the horizon from Charikot, we could see clearly into the mountain range. At this time of year, it was cold but crisp and clear with the potential for fantastic views. It was also unlikely for the trail to be crowded or busy.

We started out in Charikot initially planning to get a bus for a few hours to Singati and then walk to Chetchet and Simagaon. It was while we were waiting around near the bus stop in the bazaar that we met Thunda Sherpa, a portly middle-aged man who happened to live in Simagaon and was on his way back home in a jeep. After a glass of tea, we decided to share a jeep with him to the trailhead at Chetchet. In previous years the walk from Singati to Chetchet had been described to me as one of the most beautiful trails in all of Nepal, carved along the banks of the Tamakoshi. Now the new road which carries industrial equipment and infrastructure to serve the hydropower at Lama Bagar has destroyed any semblance of serenity. In our jeep, we passed Ganga, the site of another new hydropower project under construction. Yet at the time of our trip due to union problems work had been halted for months. This meant we drove past something that had the feel of an abandoned workshop situated on the side of a road. Old trucks, lorries and machinery, some from India, some from China, littered the side of the road. All vehicles, diggers and trucks were in various states of disrepair and abandonment. The road also churned up an immense amount of dust, giving the bedraggled town an extra gritty feel. With the heat of the hills and the dust from the road, taking the jeep was no real hardship, I wouldn't have been wanting to be walking through this. That was until we got a reckoning of just how precarious the road actually would turn out to be.

The road had been following the river for the last hour and was cut deep into the hillside. The road varied in height, at times it was level with the river, times it was a hundred metres above it. As we climb, from my seat on the right of the jeep I could see that the slope the road was held up on, looked more like a pile of dirt than something able to withhold the weight of a road. Yet we continued to make good speed in our jeep and overtook several local buses. A large part of the road was being reconstructed where previous landslides had hit and destroyed the road. We arrived at one section where we could hear some sort of commotion going on outside. Looking down to the riverbank beneath me I saw construction workers stop & look directly above our jeep, point, shout and then promptly run away. The next second a barrage of stones and rocks crashed onto the roof of the jeep. As the rocks poured down on the vehicle the driver struggled to get the jeep started again. We frantically rolled up the windows of the backseats as small rocks started to bounce their way in. After eventually getting the jeep's engine restarted we made it through scared but otherwise unscathed. Afterwards, looking behind the jeep, it became obvious that the roads really are cut and blasted into the hillsides, with very little purpose or support. It doesn't take too many of these incidents for driving to feel rather precarious.

It was another hour before we limped, the jeep battered and bruised into Chetchet. This is where we left the road behind and would not see it again until our return in a weeks' time. There was little of interest to see here and we were eager to start climbing. We start the trail to Simigaon. After crossing a small suspension bridge over the Tamakoshi, the trail began sharply with steps cut into the rock which took us steeply up for almost eight hundred metres. It was here that the entrance to the hidden valley begins. I thought back to a description I had read in one of the few guidebooks of the area.

"The entrance to the valley is marked by the sacred 'footprint' of a wandering Buddhist priest, left on the steep slope between the bridge over the Tama Koshi and Simigaon."

Yet today, having crossed the Tamakoshi, I looked around for the footprint but could not find it.

Simigaon is located almost directly vertically up from Chechet, or it at least felt like it. The trail was narrow and hugged the face of the cliff, with stone steps painfully cut into the rock. The steep climb offers no respite and despite the sun, some steps are notoriously greasy. Looking behind I noticed a worrying absence of guardrails, I did not make that mistake again. We climbed up the trail for around an hour until we reached Simigaon, a small town sprawled out amongst the terraces. Here whilst catching our breath and speaking to Thunda, we got our first look at the village. The remnants of the previous year's earthquake were clearly visible here, with the majority of people living in houses and huts constructed after the earthquake, made predominately of rocks, salvaged wood and tin sheeting. Thunda showed us his old house, an old guesthouse and the former village school, now a motley collection of rubble in varying states of decay and disrepair. There was an unmistakeably sad air to the town. It was not particularly attractive, nor charming although this may be due to the destruction and the incoming cloud which had wafted over the rubble and added a gloomy feel to proceedings. Now the afternoon wind had picked up. While huge amounts of aid had poured into Nepal after the earthquake, ten months on Simigaon looked and felt like it had been left behind. The patchwork quilt of tarpaulins with either a faded USAID or DFID logo was the only indicator of any aid reaching the town at all. The town stretched out

Photo 13: With Thunda outside his house

wide over terraces and fields. We traipsed aimlessly around the village, past and over rubble.

It was while walking around Simigaon that we got one of the biggest shocks of the trip. All of a sudden an almighty deep blast echoed around the valley, we immediately looked up on the lookout for the landslide that caused the noise. Thunda laughed, it was just the blasting they are doing in Lama Bagar hydropower. Ever since the earthquake, such noises have taken on increased importance. Feeling equally relieved and foolish we moved on now following Thunda. We came across the old campsite in Simigaon, which closed its doors after being destroyed in the earthquake and its remains now lie scattered across a field. As a result, we ended up pitching our tent outside Thunda's house while the rain came in, quickly followed by snow on the higher hills. With our tent up we joined Thunda in his house for dinner. Grateful to be indoors we ate and drank numerous cups of tea in his house before we returned to our tent for an early night with the aim to reach Beding, snow dependent, the next day.

Dogang

Waking early the next morning and emerging from our tent, we saw the snow had all but melted, apart from right on the hilltops where it remained defiant. By the time we had drunk our tea and collapsed our tent, the early morning clouds had cleared and we were left with a beautifully clear crisp morning, the sun glistening off the snow-covered hills. Before leaving and with promises of chang upon our return, Thunda gave us the name of a family member in Beding he recommended we stay with, if necessary.

It wasn't long until we were on our way, following the trail which conveniently started only a few metres behind Thunda's house. From Simigaon to Surmuche, we left the terraces and climbed steeply along an exposed ridgeline before the trail disappeared into the woods. The forest was a thick green, with dark moss covering the rocks, which contrasted sharply with the deep blue of the river below. Stone steps carved into the mountainside made up the majority of the initial trail which penetrated right through the forest. On the left side of the Rolwaling valley, we saw a small village directly opposite us; or rather we heard it before we could see it. Loud music, shouting and singing, and another stranger, possibly alcohol induced, sounds could be heard, and it was not even eight in the morning.

The trail carried up high on the right side of the valley, with trees swallowing up the views of the river at the bottom, allowing you to look only straight ahead or behind. The deeper we walked and ascended into the valley; the hills started to give way to mountains. Trees turned into sparse vistas, too steep for major vegetation or trees to grow. As the wind picked up, barrelling off all sides of the valley and the temperature began to drop we knew we are leaving the hills behind. The valley, hemmed in either side by mountains, boasted some stunning waterfalls that would later only be surpassed by the frozen waterfalls higher up. We continued to walk along the path, flanked by rhododendrons and juniper bushes. The trail was steep and our bags were heavy but not exhaustingly so. We passed several old animal huts, now empty. Across the gorge of the river, I saw a small cave nestled halfway up a cliff edge. There, I could scarcely believe lay a Shiva trident and what looked like vermilion smeared on the wall of the cave. Someone, somehow, managed to make a mandir here. At first glance, it is completely inaccessible. The cliff was incredibly steep and walking up to it would be next to impossible. Yet I can start to slowly make out the difference in the colour of rock and noticed a small trail snaking its way sporadically over the cliff, leading from the river below up to the shrine. Halfway down the trail, I spotted several blankets, arranged as if they had been left out to dry. There were enough blankets for them to have only been from someone living nearby, maybe in the cave itself. The home of a sadhu perhaps?

We stopped in Surmuche for lunch and over a lunch of chow chow and stale bread and cheese that we fished out from our bags, the lady running the shop told us of a few guests she had just a week ago. '*There was a group of 4 guys, from Kathmandu, who came for the night. I think they were on their way to Tso Rolpa too. They ate here and spent the night. The next day, I found out they'd left early in the morning without paying'.* The lady was probably in her forties. She wore an old battered kurta, with a Khukuri dangling from her waist, always within reach. She'd been chopping wood when we arrived and by the looks of the scars and callouses on her hands and the size of her shoulders, I wouldn't want her looking for me to settle an unpaid bill. *'Ah but my husband will be back from the bazaar in a few days. He should be back when they return'.* There was, after all, only one main route out of the valley. Leaving an unpaid bill in a small valley was hardly the smartest thing to do. Maybe the group had bigger things to worry about than just the wife.

After lunch at Surmuche we continued. The trail wove its way through the forest, with the river now never leaving our side. The trail undulated up and down, and the surface changed continually from the moss and root of the forests large hardwoods to the gravel and loose broken rock left behind from a falling boulder. At times, when a river crashed down from high on its way to the Rolwaling River at the bottom, we crossed a number of old worn, rickety ridges. It was four hours before we got to Kalche before continuing on for another twenty minutes to end up down in Dogang. Dogang was a beautiful little settlement consisting merely of a few houses, animal shelters and two small guest houses, of which only one was open, right at the bottom of the valley on the riverbank. After crossing several precarious bridges, with very dubious engineering and crossing makeshift paths across landslides hundreds of metres high, it was good to be on relatively safe ground. We had aimed to push onto Beding that day. However after we had spoken to several locals returning from Beding who said they'd been walking through snow up to knee height, we decided to stay in Dogang and hope the early morning sun would melt the snow before our arrival. Not being adequately prepared for several days walking through snow, we were grateful for the excuse to lie-in the next day and wait for the sun.

Unlike in Kathmandu, where the sound of buses, dogs and horns continue throughout the night, the only sound we could hear was the rush of the Rolwaling River, slowly making its way to lead into the Bhotekoshi, only several feet from where we slept.

Beding

Leaving Dogang the trail started out a lot flatter than yesterday, the first hour mixed gradual climbing with flat walks along the river bank through the by now familiar dense green trees. The air was thick with the smell of tree sap and damp soil and vegetation. For anyone who lives in Kathmandu, the smells and sounds of nature came as a welcome respite. It was a cool, crisp morning with a clear sky. Far away from the pollution of the capital, fresh and almost alpine. We greedily inhaled the mountain air.

Passing through settlements and seeing the customary mane stones and prayer flags, the link of historical trade from the valley with Tibet is clear and has played an important role in Rolwaling's history. Yak convoys would journey onto Tibet through Menlung la. In fact, Beding and Na's grazing pastures would be used by Yak convoys on their way down to the lower plains. Interestingly while trade with Tibet may have been highly lucrative in Dolakha, it hadn't always been so welcome in other parts of the country. Back in the Malla Kingdom of Kathmandu, according to Bahadur Bista, in 1650

"King Siddhinarsingh Malla decreed that anyone who had travelled to Tibet, the remaining stronghold of Buddhism, had to be purified on his return. This step stimulated a process of alienation from Tibet which had contributed so much to Nepali prosperity by of trade in the past. Merchants engaging in Tibetan trade were subjected to humiliating rites as they were regarded as impure by the Hindu high caste people."

Although these actions may be more to do with Siddhinarsingh's devotion to religion as opposed to a nationwide shift away from Tibet. After all

"Sidddhinarsinghs Hinduism and fatalistic faith were so fervent that he eventually abdicated his throne and disappeared to become a Sannyasi."

Now the trade with Tibet is all but dead, the salt caravans have long ceased to cross. The inhabitants of the valley are one of the last reminders of this trade.

After an hour, the trail turned and we entered the next stage of the valley, we were again beckoned on by the lofty peaks of the Himalayas. Surrounded almost on all sides by their dominating and almost intimidating height, we kept walking further from the foothills and into the himal proper. While the sun was out the vibrant blue of the river and the sky contrasted with the incredible white of the mountain tops. It was not long after this, however, that it started to snow, and the realization soon came that being so far up into the mountains, the success of this trip was entirely dependent upon the weather. With the clouds picking up, the peaks of Chekigo and neighbouring mountains disappeared as quickly as they had appeared. We had gambled on the weather and snow level this time of year. February was often a time of harsh winter storms, maybe our luck would run out.

During the last hour to Beding, the snow and wind picked up and our progress had quickly become a struggle. The valley acted as a wind tunnel, offering no respite from the wind. Then, through the thick clouds that hit us, we came across the remains of a small village and the biggest landslide we had seen on the trip. Not a single house or building in its path had been able to offer any significant resistance against its relentless and destructive march downwards. Picking our way through stones, boulders the sizes of cars, broken window frames and parts of houses was a sobering experience. It was almost impossible to imagine the lay of the town, it was that badly destroyed. With the mist and gloom surrounding us, it wasn't long before we were cold and soon feeling tired. The ascent had started to catch up with us. With visibility only a few feet away we turned our heads to the ground and plodded, slowly on. It wasn't much longer after that we arrived in Beding.

Beding, a Sherpa town, was littered with huge mane stones, large boulders with Buddhist inscriptions carved into the rock face that marked our arrival. Passing the Rolwaling Sangag Choling Monastery, we were told there were almost 35 households in Beding, yet in total, we maybe saw 10 people, none of them males of working age. Like so many other places in Nepal, Beding was bereft of men. With many working in India or in the Gulf. The lack of people, certainly when the weather turned nasty, gave the whole area a kind of deserted atmosphere. Our arrival into Beding also appeared to coincide with the point where waterfalls ceased to run and instead became frozen waterfalls, the lack of sound even running water added to the feeling of isolation and remoteness. The only sound to be heard was the wind whipping its way over the rock and rushing through the valley. Beding used to have communication via satellite phones but they stopped working many months ago and to date, no one had been up to fix it. The lack of communication in the villages only added to the slight feeling of abandonment that had been gnawing away at me. Certainly, the Rolwaling Valley felt miles away from the relative hustle and bustle from its two adjacent Valleys, Langtang to the west and the Solukhumbu to the east.

The first expedition in the Rolwaling valley dates back to 1951 and added a sense of mountaineering history to the region. This trip was undertaken by Eric Shipton on a reconnaissance mission to scout out potential routes up Everest. The very same trip was also where photographs of the Yeti's footprints were taken and would go onto start one of the biggest debates in mountaineering folklore regarding the existence of the elusive and fabled Yeti. After extensive exploration of the Solukhumbu, the team decided to return to Kathmandu via Gauri Shanker and the as yet unexplored or at least by Western expeditions, Rolwaling valley. It was here after crossing the Tashi Lapsa pass, following the discovery and naming of Melungtse, the highest peak in the Rolwaling valley, the team apparently discovered animal tracks that were too large to be attributed to any animal. These became the iconic Yeti footstep photographs and kick-started the debate about the Yeti's existence. Although as Shipton was a known joker, the origin of the footprints is more likely to be from an ice axe than a Yeti. Since the 50s, Rolwaling has received relatively little attention, it is this combination of a connection to mountaineering history without the hordes of the Khumbu that made the valley such an attractive choice to explore.

As we walked through Beding and saw no people I was reminded of a description of the Rolwaling Sherpas from the 1950s that I found in the first few pages of Ruebi Baumgartners Farewell to the Yak and Yeti, by far the most authoritative work in the region. In these pages was listed an extract from Tom Wier the leader of the Scottish Rolwaling Expedition of 1952, who wrote

"How tough these Rolwaling Sherpas were we later discovered; indeed they were not ordinary men and women but of the stuff, heroes are made. Little did we know as we looked them over in their baggy homespuns and Tibetan boots that they were rock climbers of whom any mountaineering club might be proud- except that no members of any mountaineering club known could do what they did."

These words are no longer true, in fact, the valley is now well known in mountaineering circles for the high quality of mountaineers that it produces. If for nothing else these days over 29 Everest summiteers can call Beding their hometown.

We had aimed to make it to Na that day, however, upon arrival in Bedding we were told it was too early in the season and no-one was currently in Na. Faced with the decision of another 2 hours walk to camp, potentially having to pitch our tent deep in snow and cook on our gas stove, or staying in Beding and being able to get warm food, we made the rather easy decision to stay in Beding. It was only whilst having dinner we realised the family we were staying with was, in fact, the family that Thunda had meant for us to get in contact with. We attacked the rice, dal and the chewy old meat with hungry intent.

It was earlier that day while entering Beding we had encountered two women working in the field, planting potatoes. They looked like a grandmother and grandchild. They told us they had a place to stay and food. We were ravenously hungry and were craving meat. Herman asked them if they had any.

'*Yes we have some meat*', the grandmother shouted back

'*What meat? Chicken or buff*' Herman replied, we both hoped that it was not a goat, comparatively very expensive.

'*Cow*' shouts back the women deadpan

Before we can reply, the grandchild with a worried look on her face adds, '*No no, not cow, she means buff*'. Illegal cow slaughter was a big deal in Nepal, with two years in jail the stated penalty. Yet here, with next to no government presence, and certainly no Shiv Sena, we were fine. Pretending that the old women made a mistake and had in-fact meant to say buff, we followed the granddaughter, now striding ahead of us, to her house and most importantly towards her chulo.

The lack of development in the area is clear and matches Rolwalings description as an area unspoilt. Interestingly the valley has long attracted those looking for undeveloped and unspoilt areas, in Baumgartner's book a survey of foreign trekkers in the valley in 1977 found that

> "in the course of these interviews the trekking tourists rated negative impacts of tourism in Rolwaling Valley significantly higher on their list of concerns than the lack of medical care of poverty'. This is probably due to their 'understandable fear of losing the privilege of exclusively consuming a pristine natural environment with a culturally authentic local set up while being fully aware that touristic impacts would transform both into a commodity over time."

Forty years later, I realise little has changed and we suffer from the same desires. Rolwaling is crying out for development, yet that same development may rob it of its charm, but preserving it as a living museum of undisturbed mountain life was neither fair, not my decision to make.

That evening with not much else to do, we got ready for an early start the next day to Na and Tso Rolpa, yet as with so many things here, it would all depend upon the weather. It was clear we would have a relatively easy day. If it snowed, however, we could well be in trouble.

Tso Rolpa

With our alarms set for five, we awoke early the next day and set the stove to boil water for coffee. However, our early start had to be delayed as it was still pitch black outside. We could see thick black clouds and feared the worst. Grateful for the imposed extra rest, we lay fully clothed with our bags packed in bed for half an hour before the sky started to light up. Reluctantly we left our warm beds for the icily cold winter dawn. Slightly delayed but finally, on our way to Na, we were greeted by a stunning sight. It had snowed again overnight, but not heavily. Today the early morning weather was fantastic and there was not a cloud in the sky. The trail left Beding and continued to head up through the narrowing valley. As the early morning sun hit the upper echelons of the Himalayas, the light radiated its way back through. What had not been clear to us in yesterday's cloud and snow became immediately apparent. We knew that Beding was nestled in the bottom of the valley, hemmed in by high hills at all sides. What we didn't know is how soon these hills gave way to behemoths that dominated the skyline. One such mountain was the sacred Gauri Shanker, which appeared behind us as 7134 metres of glistening white Himalaya. With Gauri (Shiva) and Shanker (Parvati) calling it their home. Looking from right to left, our necks craned as we tried to take just several of the 50 peaks over 6000 metres in the valley. As we look up at Gauri Shanker I remember reading about Shiva's wrathful vengeance and anger. Allegedly his presence made it hard for expeditions to summit its peak, with it not being first summited until 1979, almost 20 years after the first permits had been granted. One reason for that maybe well is the anger of the mountains sacred inhabitants. A local legend listed in my guidebook went,

"The local people believe that Gauri continually intervenes in order to prevent the might Shanker from drifting off into unreachable transcendence. A contemporary tales tells how she keeps a vigilant eye while her consort is meditating on the mountaintop. Gauri sees a group of humans toiling up towards the lofty spot where she and Narayan are seated. 'My lord', she cried, 'an expedition of mountaineers is approaching'

'How dare they come near me' Thunders Narayan in a towering rage, 'with a flick of my fingers I shall send an avalanche to destroy them!'

Gauri placates him, 'Let them come a little closer. I want to see the colour of the leader's eyes' as the expedition struggles higher, Narayan becomes more and more indignant. 'They're disturbing my peace and quiet. I will blow mighty winds to sweep them away.'

'Just let them come a little further', pleads Gauri, 'so that I can see the colour of his eyes. Oh, he is so handsome. His eyes are blue. Now, my lord, you can do as you will.'

And Shanker sends death to the climbers"

It is maybe unsurprising then why it took almost 20 years for the mountain to be successfully conquered.

It was in one such a moment when having stopped simply to remind ourselves of where we were, a hawk soared down in front of us. It could have been a goshawk or sparrowhawk but I could not be sure. With a bird of prey floating above us and snowy peaks all around us, we knew we were firmly back in the Himalayas. For almost one hour with no snow incoming, the trail continued to follow the river before we climbed again, onto a plateau in the valley. In the near distance, we could see a small settlement, Na, and behind that the rise of what could only be the banks of Tso Rolpa.

An hour and a half later we arrived at the edges of Na, yet we were presented with a problem. The entrance to Na was a small trail, wide enough for two people to walk comfortably side by side, hemmed in on either side by dry stone walls. The trail then began to narrow as it entered Na, ending up as a small single-track footpath. On either side of the trail, small plots of land were divided into plots for farming. Ordinarily, this entrance would have been fine and unnoteworthy, was it not for the fifteen yaks down the trail, blocking our entrance.

I'd seen Yaks before, but they were predominate, Zopkios or Dzums, male and female hybrid breeds, a cross between a Yak and a Buffalo. They were often crossbred for producing hardy animals for grazing lower down the mountain. These, however, were pure thoroughbreds. The nearest, twenty metres away, was huge and looked aggressive, hunched up on his stocky shoulders, I looked over worryingly at Herman, only for him to look back at me, equally concerned.

'Do you fancy it?' he asked

'Not a chance' I replied.

Out here, we hadn't seen anyone else all day. This was not the time to risk serious injury and to be gored by a Yaks horns, trapped between two walls. Yaks, after all, were notoriously aggressive, and immensely strong. Agonizingly slowly, we climbed the stone walls and made our way behind the main entrance to Na, walking behind the Yaks in a rather undignified entrance into Na.

Walking into Na we caught the familiar taste of abandonment, with everyone in Na living at a lower altitude waiting for the trekking and farming season to begin, Baumgartner states that

> "During the winter months, Rolwaling Sherpas live scattered over no less than four settlement clusters between 3,200 and 3,400 metres. Social interaction becomes limited to the few neighbouring households."

This was clear to see and we had the town completely to ourselves, apart from the numerous groups of Yaks that is. Similar to Beding, walking through a village with numerous households but no people or signs of life was a slightly surreal experience.

We ate our lunch on the banks of the river that flows from Tso Rolpa's banks down past Na. We tucked into the bread and cheese we'd been carrying since Charikot. Luckily the cold nights had kept the cheese edible but the bread was hard and stale. Yet sitting down, drinking ice cold glacial water flanked on three sides by mountains tantalisingly close, I did not think of the stale bread. Earlier that month, sitting around the fire in Herman's resort, we had heard tales of a Nepali skiing group coming to Na for practice. I could now see the slope they'd used, a cruel few hundred metres above Na. With the walk here, plus additional agonising climb in ski boots for each run down, I didn't think backcountry skiing at four thousand metres would catch on. The run they had, from here at least, hardly looked worthwhile.

Leaving Na in our ascent to Tso Rolpa, we crossed the river and began walking across the snow-covered flat ground that separated Na from the banks of the largest Glacial Lake in Nepal. Now the altitude started to kick in as we both struggled on. Yet our efforts were rewarded when the sheer scale of where we soon became apparent. We were no longer walking around the Himalaya but in them. With approaches to peaks veering off from our path, with the

Photo 14: Herman in front of the Rolwaling Valley

right ropes and equipment we could have easily bagged several
peaks. After a long trudge from Na, we eventually reached the bottom
of the banks of Tso Rolpa. Tso Rolpa is not only the largest Glacial
Lake in Nepal, but it is also in an increasingly precarious state.
Considered at high risk of Glacial Lake Outburst Flooding, the banks
had been reinforced a few years ago and early warning systems put in
place. Boulders lined its banks, with a path skipping over frozen ice
and rock dragging us to the top. Although at this stage the
development and reinforcement on the banks of the lake didn't seem
reassuring enough to us as we dragged ourselves up to the final
ascent. Starting at the valley bottom at Chetchet only 3 days before
had not left us not fully acclimatised. Therefore it would be
disingenuous to describe the final section of climbing almost 200
metres of steep vertical as anything more than an ordeal. Wheezing
we dragged our heavy legs up the path, on our final ascent. The
respite was that every 10 metres we were offered a new view of a
mountain that had come into view. The final steps carved into the
rock were covered in snow, but eventually, after 3 days and 3000
metres of vertical climbing we climbed over the last boulder and Tso
Rolpa finally came into view.

The shimmering white hue of the lake fed by the Trakarding Glacier, which was completely frozen, could only be matched by the surrounding peaks. The lake was surrounded by white encroaching glaciers. Looking behind into the Rolwaling valley, it looked as if we had left civilisation behind. My guidebook told me

'Buddhists believe it to be a 'hidden land' or beyul, where Tibetan Buddhism can always be protected and revitalised, even in the face of challenges from the outside world.'

Right then I understood, we were in the Rolwaling beyul. By this stage, the early morning sun had really come out in force, and the magnificent blue sky could be found deep in the glacial ice and in glaciers close to 1000 metres above us. Walking, tentatively, onto the frozen lake it was impossible not to smile, surrounded by nothing but mountains and extreme terrain on all sides we were reminded just of the small scale of our human lives and the sheer indomitable power of nature. From Tengi Ragi Tau to Bigphera Go Shar, we were surrounded by peaks. We seemed so small and insignificant in the face of such massifs. As I left my footprints upon the lake's frozen surface it cracked and a deep rumble echoed around us; it had the sound and depth and tone of an avalanche. Above us, lay overhanging glaciers, rock falls and precious peaks.

To the right of me lay a government monitoring station and the start of the early warning system that in the case of a glacial lake outburst flood would alert all the residents downstream. Except now the alarm posts were empty, having been liberated of their batteries and solar panels by the Maoists. To the left, over Herman's shoulder, I could see into mountain ranges in Tibet. Once again, I found myself staring into the Tibetan Autonomous Region. Ever close, yet forever far away.

With us both knowing that within a few days of continuing our trek we would cross the Tashi Lapek pass and drop down into

Photo 15: Standing on top of a frozen Tso Rolpa

Namche Bazaar in the Solukhumbu, it was with no small reluctance we realised our onward journey had to end here. We had already spent an hour at Tso Rolpa, it was now nine in the morning and the sun had long been out. Despite the snow, there was not a lot of wind, and the heat had picked up. It was serene and apart from the occasional rumblings of the ice, deathly quiet. Looking around, my eyes skirted between peaks and passes and each wandering of my irises was rewarded. We walked over to the house containing the early warning system for the rest of the valley. It was a small stone building, somehow with a vehicle inside, presumably carried up by helicopter. Only protected by a single barbed wire fence, which we easily ducked under. The warning system wasn't reassuring, but the fact that we knew it didn't work clearly didn't help.

We slowly started to head back to Na, we were by now hungry and wanted to head down for some warm food and hot tea. The icy path which had been frustrating on the way up now became treacherous upon the way down. Our boots slipped and we constantly fought for purpose on the sheet ice hidden in the shade. With our hands out, looking to grab nearby rocks for stability, we slowly picked our way down the trail, until halfway down, mercifully the ice rescinded and we were back walking again on rock and grass. The ascent, which took us almost an hour to plod up, was quickly dispatched on the return journey in twenty minutes, every step down from 4400 metres filling our lungs with newly found oxygen. With the climbing over, losing altitude and having achieved the major priority of the trip, the steps were the easiest they'd been so far on the trip.

Relaxed and complete with feelings of achievement we ambled our way back to Na, talking, planning future trips and inevitably constantly commenting on the scenery. Luckily, when we found ourselves crossing the metal bridge back into Na, the Yaks from before had dispersed all around Na and we could, in fact, walk through the town without risk. There were a few trekking lodges, inevitably with the windows plastered with the logos of various trekking organisations and companies from around the world. Numerous Nepali and Sherpa groups were on display as was a patchwork of European countries represented from Sweden, Czech Republic, France, Germany and Italy. Yet there was no-one here, and the lodge had been boarded up for the season. The decision to stay last night in Beding had been a good one. But it did mean we had an hour trudge back down to Beding for some lunch, before heading further back down the valley. It was now Thursday, and I had to be back in Kathmandu for work on Monday. As much as it would have been nice to explore the beyul further, I had a bus to catch on Sunday morning back from Charikot.

Herman and I walked on and now we left Na behind, and with constant glances, over our shoulder, the banks of Tso Rolpa slowly disappeared around the curvature of the valley. Twenty minutes later, so did Na. The clouds were starting to gather, and the wind picked up, whipping around the valleys V-shaped slopes. Walking into the wind we started to tire again and hoped that this was not the first signs of the returning snow. Our water was finished, as was our food. While Beding was less than an hour away, we were making a meal of it. Then, coming towards us we saw a lone man, walking up the trail with a huge backpack and what looked like eight-foot high trekking poles. More strangely, he was European and alone. Our paths crossed and we exchanged pleasantries. This was, after all, the first foreign trekker we had seen since leaving Kathmandu. The man was around 40, with a sunburnt nose and lips caked in embalmer. Despite the climb, he was breathing calmly and apart from a thin line of perspiration on his forehead, there were little signs of physical exhortation. We asked him where he was going. *'I'm off to Na, for a month. There is some fantastic bouldering up there. I'm hoping to improve some aspects of my technique. Then I was thinking of going over the Tashi Lapsa and flying back from Namche'* he replied in a thick French accent. Coming to Nepal and spending a month at almost four thousand metres alone to practise bouldering technique it was clear he was a dedicated climber. He was obviously one of the more serious and eccentric mountaineers that Rolwaling attracted. He went on to say that his porter was below him and someone would be coming up to Na to open a lodge for him. Yet, even if not alone, a month in windy desolate Na was not for the light-hearted. Sherpas used this place to train for Himalayan expeditions, a mixture of challenging climbing, proximity to the Khumbu and an absence of crowds. We left the man on his way to Na, and he too was soon swallowed into the mist, almost as if he had been an apparition.

Crossing a stream we saw the outline of Beding appear thankfully in the distance. Ten minutes later we were relieved. Dropping our bags down and stretching our legs in the kitchen of our lodge we saw again a new visitor. Next, to the fire, there was a thirty-year-old Nepali trekking guide, and next to her a woman of around 25, French too, as it later turned out. We hadn't seen anyone for days and now two Frenchmen in the space of twenty minutes. We joined them by the fire as the lodge owner prepared some chow-chow and tea. She was a student from Lyon and was in Nepal for a few weeks and wanted to go trekking, but somewhere a little different and she had heard about this place from a friend's father. Yet they'd arrived that morning from Kalche and she was too tired to want to engage in much conversation.

The guide, on the other hand, was in his element. Now with a crowd of people willing to listen, or too tired to put up any resistance, he told tales from previous trips and was boisterously happy to have someone to listen to him. The girls English had been in an almost impregnable French accent, and his English wasn't amazing either. Unsurprisingly I reckoned they not been striking up much of a conservation together. He was happy to talk, although when he said this was his first time in Rolwaling, let alone as a guide I and Herman shared a wry glance.

After our chow chow, we laced our boots up, looked at Beding one last time before heading down, on what we hoped would just be a few hours down to Dogang, and a beer with our feet in the river ahead of us we set off. The trip up from Dogang had been a steep climb, and straight away the descending took a toll on our tired knees. Without trekking poles to steady ourselves our knees took the brunt and soon become sore and unsteady. Yet, in our haste to descend we had forgotten much about the journey up and had forgotten how much the trail undulated cruelly in altitude, there was still a lot of climbing to do. The trail dragged on, our talking turned to sporadic comments before ceasing altogether. Our pace slowed as we tired. By now it was five p.m. and was already starting to get dark. In February, daylight was all too often fleeting and we both knew how fast it could get really dark. Not wanting to pitch a tent, and with our eyes firmly set on beer and rice we ploughed on, heads to the ground.

When finally we stumbled into Dogang in thick dusk, we saw joyfully that the lights were on and the old lady who looked after us last time is outside peeling potatoes and she greets us with a smile. Our legs were shaky and our backs groaning under the weight of our backs, but we had made it just before sunset.

Sitting, with our much thought about beer, by the river we reflected on our trip. The next day we hoped to make it down to Simigaon where we had arranged to be picked up in a jeep and head back to Charikot. The day after that, I would continue on to Kathmandu. We had walked almost twelve hours that day, from Beding to Na and Tso Rolpa and back down past Beding to Dogang. There had been a lot of altitude change and we were exhausted.

I looked left, back up the valley to where we had come. By now, the setting sun had cast darkness high in the sky but I could still see a few hundred metres ahead of me. The remnants of the sun, behind us, illuminated the mountain ridge high above the river. The colour fractured into different shades of dark dusty orange, even pink, wrestling for sight with the clouds. Below as the rock gave way to the tree line as the branches rocked steadily in the wind. An eagle, or hawk, I could never tell the difference, flew over the newly found moss and juniper bushes before rising over the crest of the river and disappearing out of sight.

I shivered and wasn't sure why.

Simigaon

The next morning, we were heralded out of bed by another clear sky. With a simple thousand metres descent over trail we knew, and a jeep waiting at the bottom, the morning had a light jovial feel. We both knew that the hard work was over and there was no new trail to break and with luck, a warm shower was waiting at the end of the day. Heading on a path we already knew was one of the problems I had with A to B treks, once you arrived you merely headed back and turned around the way you came. This robbed you of some extra things to see, or at least some new terrain to explore on the return journey.

We sat, at almost eight in the morning, our latest start so far of the trip and ate Tibetan bread and jam and washed it all down with some coffee. There was just us, the woman and her grandchild who on close inspection looked *bahulo* too, and the odd goat. It was a beautiful spot, and the small wooden animal huts surrounding us leant a rustic charm to the area, although I knew just a month ago this place would have been verging on inhospitable due to the winter snow.

Downing our coffee, and with promises to return, we picked up our bags for the last time and made our way down to Simigaon and ultimately home back to Kathmandu. Now trail fit and with the most of the food now eaten our packs felt lighter than they had on the whole trip and we made good speed, eager for a warm shower, clean socks and cold beer in Charikot. As a result, it was not long before we arrived into Kalche, that was yet again deserted. Stopping only for a drink of water we continued our way down. The trail re-entered the forest and for the last time, the glistening Himalayan peaks disappeared from view. We were back in the hills. To accompany us, we saw more cows, goats and chickens than we had during the last few days and the smells of vegetation and the unmistaken smell of animal excrement greeted us back into the fertile hills of Nepal. Farmers started to appear both above and below the trail. When we heard the mobile radio of village child playing we knew we were home.

For lunch, we placed our packs down in Surmuche. The woman was still there, still chopping wood. She confirmed, yes her husband had arrived back from the Bazaar, but those guys hadn't returned. With neither me nor Herman able to guess where they could have disappeared to, we ate our lunch in silence.

The last of the bread was used up, and the cheese, now semi-solidified was equally promptly dispatched off. Herman's used the woman's phone to call the hotel to send a car down for us. It would take the car around two hours to get to Chechet and us about the same.

The trail now may almost not have been there, our conversation was of life and things back in Kathmandu civilisation. We discussed what our next weekend plans were and it was as if we had already mentally left the Rolwaling valley, although our feet still left imprints on its path.

After one final climb, the falling terraces of Simigaon appeared and as we picked our way down, we watched fifteen villagers cumulatively plough a field, while one man tried to attach the plough to a very uncooperative buffalo. It was good to see life again, and I noticed, working men not just females. The sounds of the village carried over to us and with the sun high in the sky, it was with great ease we walked, as if triumphant, through Simigaon. Reaching the end of the village we saw the river below us emerge, and after a final descent, the road back home lay nestled at the bottom of the valley.

By now the clouds had come in and it started to rain. Not heavily but enough to make the stone steps, so difficult on the way up, now overtly slippery and precarious on the way down. Going slowly, not wanting to break an ankle fifteen minutes from the end we slowed our pace and eventually made it down to the river. We looked back up behind us, but any sights we had hoped to see were dwarfed and blocked by the cliff we'd just climbed down. Our trip in the Rolwaling valley had come to a close and we were soon rather unceremoniously back down on the banks of the Tamakoshi. Walking over the bridge, and walking the last few metres up to the road, the jeep came into view. Our time in the Rolwaling valley had been equally challenging and rewarding. With an atmosphere like no other in Nepal, the valley was truly special. To say the Rolwaling valley is an intoxicating combination of being both unspoiled and unique, would be a horrible and worn out cliché, yet it would also be true.

We may be leaving the wide valley, but I would long think back to its windswept sides, its moody skies and of the wind howling around Rolwaling, its sound is immediately swallowed up by the walls of the valley. If a valley had to give birth to the rise of the myth Yeti, it is fitting it was here. A moody seldom seen creature, steeped in legend and revealing itself to few. It was fitting indeed.

Eastern Nepal

The Eastern Terai

I had left early, in an attempt to beat the morning traffic, and it wasn't long before I had passed Bhaktapur and was pulling away up past Sanga and through one of the few exit routes out the Kathmandu valley. My bike, an old Honda CBZ, was becoming increasingly ropey and now only fired on all cylinders on special occasions. I continued down the road and came through Banepa, what was supposedly a previously beautiful town, but today I could see no remnants of that beauty. The highway cut brutally through the town, a crude divide that carves the town into two. The road dominates life in Banepa. The dust flew up off the lorries, cars, bikes and trucks that plough through the town's streets. I pulled down my visor and squinted in an attempt to see through the dust. With recent unfinished road construction, being stuck behind a truck on a windy day was equivalent to being in a small sandstorm, just more polluted and with none of the romance. Battling the dust I soon arrived in Dhulikhel, another formerly prestigious town that too had lost all glamour with the intrusion of the highway. Although what Banepa and Dhulikhel have lost in their tranquillity they have gained in commerce, increased land prices and a number of business opportunities relating to the highway. There were some resorts up here but with the traffic creating significant amounts of pollution, the alluring mountain view the town commands from its location on the valley ridge is far too seldom seen. I left the Arniko Highway which continued on to Kavre, Sindhupalchowk, Dolakha and the Tibetan Border, which I have ridden so many times in the past. Instead, I turned down the BP Koirala highway. This highway, which snaked its way through the Mahabharata range to end down in Bardibas in the Terai, is named after Nepal's first Prime Minister and independence hero. In fact, BP Koirala commissioned the project when he was Prime Minister in 1959 and even laid a foundation stone down. Yet in 1960 when King Mahendra dismissed the elected government and imposed Panchayat rule, the project would be forgotten, not to be revived until 1996 with Japanese assistance. The road was frightfully expensive and it wasn't until 2015 that the highway was officially handed over to the Nepalese government. The road today, despite its long conception period, twists through the long sweeping hairpin, bends gaining and losing hundreds of metres of altitude and is well known amongst motorbike enthusiasts. Yet BP Koirala died in 1982 and would never see the road that bears his name.

The initial part of the road climbed and fell for several kilometres, with some beautiful swooping turns, but the road surface was pockmarked with potholes and haphazardly constructed speed bumps are everywhere, so it was hard to get a real rhythm on the bike going. After half an hour the road finished its descent and continued up onto a riverbank to my left and onto an elevated flood road. It was wonderful to be on the road again, and away from the dust of Kathmandu. The road was hemmed on either side by steeply climbing hills and with dotted forest coverage. The side of the road, as ever, was replete with people waiting for buses in front of houses, roadside stalls, goats and people drying wheat and peppers on the roadside and the road itself. When trucks and cars drive over the slowly drying produce the women scarcely batted an eye.

It was late April and the first round of local elections was then only three weeks away. Being the first local elections in 20 years these were of significant importance. Closer to Dhulikhel and Kathmandu, there were noticeable amounts of the red and white four starred flag of the Nepali Congress Party. These flags were invariably paired with a sister white flag, complete with a tree, the symbol of the Congress party. As a result, the party was often referred to in Nepali simply as rook, meaning tree. Now having left the larger settlements behind, after every 100 metres I was instead greeted with the hammer and sickle, the famous sign of the Maoists, or to give them their full title the Communist Party of Nepal (Maoist). For the rest of my journey, my distance would be marked by the number of Maoists flags I would pass. This blur only being disturbed by the star of the rival CPN-UML, or Communist Party of Nepal (Unified Marxist-Leninist)

The extent of campaigning was by no means limited to political bunting strung out on trees, motorbikes decked in flags and slogans plied up and down the road, often followed futilely slowly by tractors, which were also decked out in flags and party supporters. Some vehicles I noticed sported one or two speakers on the front and a passionate, or bored, a man shouting or talking lazily into the microphone, depending on how many people were about at the time. Congress and the Maoists were easily the most visible campaigners, followed by the UML and I only saw a few red and yellow striped flags with a cow in its centre, the flag of the Rastrya Pranjata Party, or RPP.

As the road wound its way south-east of Kathmandu, my vision was of pine trees which surrounded a fragmented river basin and the scent of pine leaves filled the air. The road came to its crescendo just before Khurkot, when the Japanese built road snaked, climbed and descended hundreds of metres like any mountain road in Switzerland. It is a beautiful road, but any sense of serenity is shattered by the huge tracks and the host of lorries that bare down upon you. The road only opened a few years ago, already has a poor surface, and has played host to several accidents. Tyre marks leading off the road are found next to barriers that are dented, smashed or worse, missing altogether. These are left there to serve as a grim witness. As the road reached the peak of one particularly steep climb, just before it swung right, there was a shrine built into the side of the road. Here, despite there being no real stopping point, cars and bikes had come to a standstill so people could make offerings for a safe journey. The fact that several came close to getting run over in the process did not appear to be seen as ironic.

All of a sudden, as the relatively busy highway, came to a halt, I saw a rapidly approaching queue, almost a kilometre in length and made up primarily of microbuses. The passengers were milling about, having tea and chow chow from a nearby stall placed by an entrepreneurial local woman. This signified a long wait. On the bike, I filtered between oncoming traffic on my right and the stationary microbuses on my left, before coming to the front of the queue. A small wooden shack has been hastily constructed and there sat a lone policeman, eyes barely open, while his walkie-talkie lay on the table in front of him. The highway dropped down to the left, but the way was blocked by a series of branches and rocks strewn clumsily across the road. A rough dirt road had been cut into the shoulder above the highway. Dust churned up by the oncoming traffic billowed off the diverted road. I waited at the front of the queue with the other bikes for 15 minutes. It was hot and uncomfortable but my engine deserved a rest. As I waited with the sun beating down, the sweat dripped off my brow and collated with the dust on my forehead to form a dark muddy paste. While the oncoming cars and jeeps kept appearing out of the dust I remember reading in a newspaper about this exact road collapse just a week ago. Built over almost twenty years, the road was a showcase of Japanese Nepali bilateral development. It was a phenomenally expensive project and upon completion was a real feather in the cap of the respective agencies from both Japan and Nepal. That a section had collapsed so soon, was undeniably embarrassing. The reason was, according to the article, due to the difficult terrain, the road was designed mainly for microbuses, not for the larger heavier lorries and buses that passed over the road on a daily basis, and indeed continued to do so today. As a result, a section of the road collapsed, not being designed or built for the weight that it was forced to take. Once the traffic cleared and the policeman waved the vehicles on, all the while not moving from his chair, I pulled ahead of the microbuses to my left onto the diverted road and continued down to Khurkot.

I stopped in Khurkot for food as by now my bike's engine was dangerously warm. I stopped for thali and some water. After twenty minutes I pushed on, aiming for the holy city of Janakapur, famous for the Sita Janaki temple and the home of many Hindu ascetics.

Another hour or so after Khurkot I finally left the hills behind in my mirrors and arrived in Bardibas at the end of the BP Koirala Highway. I had reached the Terai and the heat was now prickly and oppressive. After a kilometre, I'm unceremoniously dumped on the East-West Highway. I turned east and headed towards Janakapur. The highway, or Mahendra Rajamarg, started being constructed in the 1960s, yet wasn't completed until the 1970s. It was a highway that during times of political instability was of great strategic importance, especially as it allowed the king to deploy his army around the country, particularly convenient in times of civil or political unrest. Today though there is no army and the highway is instead complete with all the sights and sounds of life in the plains.

Turning off the highway after a few kilometres onto the smaller road to Janakpur I could already see the unmistakable silhouettes of Hindu pilgrims in the distance. Some walked barefoot along the road. Sometimes I passed a tractor carrying a trailer full of elderly women and I glanced at the occasional lone elderly man, relying almost heart-wrenchingly too much on his wilted old cane as he shuffled along the side of the road, tiffin box clanging noisily aside him.

Janakapur, also known as Janakpurdham was the home and capital of ancient Mithila, an important city of learning and culture and was allegedly the home of King Janak, the father of Sita. Being the adopted home of Sita, who was the consort of Rama in the great Ramayana epic, is one reason the city retains its religious significance

When I arrived it was a dusty town, full of winding and densely packed back streets. I rode through town before, following the directions of an eight year old boy I'd asked, I parked my bike on the side of the road and began walking. I was heading to see the Janaki temple, pictures of which I had seen replicated all over Nepal. I heard Hindi, Maithili and Bhojpuri but no Nepali. I saw pilgrims from all over India, people from Uttar Pradesh, Bihar, Bengal and even further afield from Karnataka and Kerala. From Nepal I saw Madheshis and Tharus, but no Pahadis. The shops that lined the streets were full of pictures of gods, goddess and scenes from the Ramayana, offerings and other knick-knacks for pilgrims. I finally came across the gates of the temple. Walking through the temple gates into the courtyard, the temple stood out from the town in both its size and the amount of space around it. The city does not cling to the temple the way it skirts and clings to its boundary walls. The temple was an off-white, the domed wonder complete with red green and blue decorations on the walls. There were domed turrets on the roof and extended ornate pink window ledges. Intricately patterned tiles lined the floor, the smell of incense was heavy in the air cloying with the air already thick with humidity. It had the defiant feel or essence of one the grand Rajput temples across northern India. While the temple may have looked old it was constructed in 1910 apparently at the exorbitant cost, at the time, of nine lakh rupees, and is a fantastic example of Rajput Nepali architecture. Its cost had not been forgotten, the temple was still occasionally referred to as the nine lakh temple.

Yet it was not the temple that my eye was immediately attracted to. There were several hundred people inside the temple complex. I saw well over a hundred, pilgrims and priests dotted along the floor. Some ascetics were lying down, their clothes spread out on the floor. Some were chanting, some were fiddling with beads, others were sleeping or merely gazing at their navel. I saw bundles of tour groups from all over India, entering the temple complex. The floors of the temple were filled with rubbish, empty boxes of matches, fruit peel, torn playing cards, the ends of incense sticks and the other assorted trash that seemed to be essential to the ambience of every Hindu temple, or at least almost everyone I'd been to. Most of the collected trash on the floor was left over from pujas and Prasad, just not the playing cards. As I approached the entrance a bored guide sat in a chair. I asked if I was allowed in, as not all temples are open to non-Hindus. He said yes. I left my shoes at the door and entered. Passing through the walls I saw another small courtyard surrounding the inner temple, I approached, passing a sign saying no photographs. My feet passed through the dirt on the floor and I let my eyes wander around the temple.

The priest, standing behind a barrier beckoned me over. He asked me in English where I am from, when I reply in Nepali he beamed and pulled a small tray from beneath the counter. Dipping his fingers into vermillion he again beckons me forward. I have never liked wearing Tikka. I am not a Hindu, nor do I have a place in the Varna's, therefore wearing tikka always seemed a form of unnecessary posturing. I tried to argue, but he insisted, looking hurt and repeating 'Prasad, Prasad, Prasad'. I leant forward thinking the sweat would wash it off soon enough anyway. His fingers touched my forehead and daubed on the Tikka. With a forehead thick of prasad I stood upright again, he pressed an old stale laddo in my hand. A treat for any pilgrim.

Behind the temple was a museum and self-described picture show. For my fifteen rupees, I was given a small stub of a ticket and

Photo 16: The Janaki Mandir

beckoned over to some stairs. I walked up the stairs into a small dark curtained room with several model recreations involving Sita and other scenes from the epic Ramayana. Unfortunately, it looked like and had the gravitas of something that had been made by school children. The plaster appeared to be in competition with the paint in which could overlap and run the most. It was undeniably cheap and tacky but here, in this setting, it seemed altogether absurd. It was as if a poorly sculpted papier-mâché model of the Mother Mary was on display at the Church of the Nativity. I went to find the museum, which was in the basement and with the marble floor looked suspiciously like an old public toilet. The smell of the room does little to dampen my suspicions. Here several dusty old cabinets are half filled with paintings and assorted memorabilia. It, like so many other museums in Nepal, was disappointing, tacky, rather uninformative, but undeniably charming. But I am not alone, the picture show and museum are thronged with pilgrims and families. I had to jostle for a good look at the exhibits. A young girl of 8 came up to me, looked at me suspiciously before asking me in Hindi where I'm from. When I replied she ran away and a woman who was probably her grandmother scowled at me.

I left the temple and retrieved my shoes. Young men sat nearby, glued to their mobile phones, elderly grandmothers doddered over carrying offerings quietly determined while young boys with their hands closed around their fathers looked bored. I stepped back out of the temple gates. Walking around the town it pulsated with energy, far from the small religious village I had read it used to be. Even only forty years ago the town was much smaller. The city has changed much since then. The esteemed Nepali scholar Dr Harka Gurung, in his Vignettes of Nepal, published first in 1980, wrote of a trip to Janakapur.

"Janakpur was a typical Tarai town with a number of rice mills and business houses...The present town is enclosed by an eight-kilometre long brick-paved ring road within which are 24 large tanks and 21 ponds, numerous Hindu shrine dedicated to Rama, Sita Laxman and Hanuman. No animal slaughter is allowed within the limits of the ring road."

Today many of the tanks and ponds remain, as do the Hindu shrines. Yet today many lie forgotten or are left to compete for attention with new buildings, bridges and mobile phone shops. There was once a train station here, the tracks running to Jayanagar in neighbouring Bihar. Alas, the railway to India is no more. Closed in 2014 for renovation it has so far yet to re-open. This is a shame as the Terai is clearly crying out for a rail link parallel to the East-West Highway.

I wandered back over to my bike and headed back to the highway. I still had an hour or two to get to Rajbiraj in Saptari and slightly wary of dacoits I wanted to arrive before dark. The road headed back through Janakpur and wound past ponds, mandirs, more shops and butchers, so it seemed some things have changed since Harka Gurung was here. The backstreets have the look, sights, sounds and smell of any village in Uttar Pradesh or Bihar. This may be Nepal, but not the Nepal that is reflected in its national identity as a Himalayan nation. Back on the road, I competed for space with overloaded lorries, all with Uttar Pradesh or Bihar plates, which swerved to avoid bullock carts equally overloaded with straw. Hero bicycles dotted the side of the road, ridden either by groups of women coming from school or men returning from work, often with another colleague perched on the luggage rack on the back of the bike.

Ever since I left the BP highway I had been travelling through the Terai, the home of the Madheshis. The Madhesh has a long and interesting history and a political one that has been difficult, complex and increasingly violent. The term Madhesh is derived from the Sanskrit term Madhya Desh, or the middle country. The region is commonly known, albeit with small geographical variations, as the land between the Himalayas and the Vindhya mountain range in Madhya Pradesh in India, below which is often considered the beginning of southern India. It was the traditional home to the Madheshis, The term Madheshi itself is reserved for those hailing from the plains of the Terai, with a shared language, religion and culture to those in the north of Indian. Yet the term Madheshi does not refer to just one homogenous group, rather a collection of Hindus, Muslims and smaller indigenous ethnic groups who have called the Terai home for centuries. While the term Madheshi may be broad, it is not inclusive of those Nepalese from the hills who migrated to the plains in search of better economic opportunities and easier to cultivate farming land.

Despite a rich historical and linguistical heritage, the Madhesh has struggled to find a place in Nepal's national identity. Living in entirely different geographical regions and having different customs, the Madhesh is an area that has long had its differences and grievances with rulers in Kathmandu. These differences have often been used and played upon, by both sides for political gain. In the words of historian John Whelpton

> *"The superior status of hillmen in the Nepalese state was made clear in the Muluki Ain (first legal document), which ranked Parbatiya Brahmans higher than Madheshi ones. Since a common sense of separation from the plains was the main thing that hill Nepalese shared, Madheshis were naturally felt to be outsiders."*

This divide has continued to be maintained, including sometimes by overt political actions, particularly by the monarchy as a crude form of divide and rule. Writing in his Battles of the New Republic, Prashant Jha, Nepali journalist for the Hindustan times summarized the exclusion of the Madheshi from the Nepali identity as a conscious and Machiavellian move by King Mahendra.

> *"He constructed a narrative in which the monarchy was the symbol of the unity of the nation. And faith in the 'glorious' history of the Shah dynasty, a common language (Nepali), a common religion (Hinduism), and a common dress (Daria-salwar) tied the country together. This definition of a 'true Nepali' immediately privileged a certain group of people- the hill Bahuns and Chehhtis- who fulfilled the above criteria"*

By portraying the Madheshis as un-Nepali, it weakened the validity of any criticisms of the Monarchy originating from the Terai.

While the Madhesh was the traditional home of the Madheshis, during the 1950s there was considerable migration of hill people who moved down to the Terai. This was state-sanctioned and new arrivals were given land by the King in a process of Nepalisation, which immediately had a big social effect. Arriving hillmen were given land to own and farm, provided they cleared the jungle first. All this was done without any local consultation or reparations. Previously the Madhesh was considered a malarial jungle. After a USAID and WHO programme in the 1950s, which dumped DDT over the jungle, the way was clear for outsiders to move in and hill people flooded in to the plains looking for cheap land that was easier to cultivate, whilst the government sat back and watched as the migration diluted regional identities.

Ideas of Nepalisation were soon put into action, schools taught in Nepali and little lip service was given to the history or culture of the Terai in school curriculums. Then encouraged by the monarchy, more and more paharias migrated down to the fertile plains of the Tarai and were given land, first by the Ranas then the monarchs in an attempt to ethnically diffuse the Madheshi stronghold on the region. Preference was also given to hill people when electing leaders. These long-standing grievances have yet to be solved and worked through, and as a result, over the last few years, the Terai has long been host to violent incidents.

Nowhere is that more apparent than where I am now. The road to Saptari passes through Lahan. Even before the events of the last few months, Lahan was already infamous. In 2007 Lahan was the location where Ramesh Mahato, an MJF protestor, was killed by Maoists on 19 January. This killing was followed by unrest, more violence and protests all over the Terai that culminated in GP Koirala, the then Prime Minister addressing the nation, expressing a commitment by the government to meet the demands of the Madhesh movement. GP Koirala and his government promised amendments of the constitution and promised the provision of citizenship certificates. To date, many of these words and promises have failed to materialise and inclusion has neither happened nor looks any nearer. In fact, the gap between the hills and the plains now looked bigger than ever. Broken promises continue to rankle and while these promises may have been long forgotten in Singha Durbar, their unfulfilled words are not forgotten in the Madhesh.

Yet it is for more recent events that I think of Lahan. It was only one month ago, that the former Prime Minister, and UML leader, KP Oli attempted to reach Lahan. He was not deemed to be welcome, particularly due to his role and perceived actions during the border blockade of 2015. Protests swelled, and tensions boiled over tragically culminating in the death of 5 civilians by police fire in March 2017.

I thought back to pictures of roadblocks haphazardly constructed following the shooting, a reminder of their presence remained today. Initially, it is only every hundred metres that I saw scarred marking burned into the road from burning tyres and oil cans. Soon there were too many to count. Thinking back to the picture of blockades I shuddered, this place, on the surface so calm exploded only a month before, and could very well in a few weeks do so again with the upcoming election. Old burned out oil cans and piles of tyres lay strewn at the side of the road, well within easily accessible reach if they are required again. For now, though, the only roadblocks and checkpoints belonged to the police. Had the bandhs been on now and enforced, with my Kathmandu plates, I'm not sure how welcome I would have been. Today though, things on the surface at least appear fine and there is little sign of the siege of the Madhesh.

The road continued in a straight line bearing down upon Khakavita and Nepal's eastern border with India, and the roads to Darjeeling. Several factories lined either side of the road. Yet these factories were not open today, nor do many looks as if they had been open for years. Many shut after the 2008 Madheshi Andolan. It was a stark reminder that even in the eastern Terai, particularly the area closer to Biratnagar and the heartland of Nepal's industry labour disputes were all too common. Today Nepal's industry looks in a sorry state. Problems relating to unions and labour strikes were all too frequent. It was often a mixture of militant, and almost universally politically affiliated labour union leaders, and poor leadership from the owners that led to these entrenched issues.

Now there were fewer Maoist flags and instead more of the green, white and red star of the Madhesi Jana Adhikar Forum. The Maoists were no friends of the Madhesh, having shared a tumultuous recent history. One particularly defining moment in this dis-relationship is the Guar incident. Indeed, half an hour later I pass Guar, the site of a massacre. Like other towns that dot the highway, there were little physical reminders that remain to remind travellers passing through of the history and stories that came out of Gaur. Yet this incident, in particular, has been etched into the consciousness of many as a reminder of one of the worse, most violent and senseless incidents of Nepal's recent political history.

On 21 March 2007, the MJF and the Maoists had staged a meeting in Guar. Both the Maoists and MJF had organised different gatherings, but somehow at the same venue and on the same day. In the weeks leading up to the event, there had been a number of clashes and tensions were high. It was reported thousands of MJF workers have arrived with sharpened bamboo sticks, while hundreds of Maoists also had improvised weapons and slingshots. Both sides were ready for violence. I leave it to Prashant Jha to relate the actions of that day and what happened next.

"No one no-one expected the brutality that followed. In the afternoon several MJF supporters, not heeding the instructions of their leaders, attacked and damaged the stage where the Maoists had gathered. The Maoists retaliated and a violent frenzy began between the Maoists, MJF and now the local police trying to calm the situation down. Shots were fired by all sides. The MJF had more men and led a brutal attack on the Maoists by the time the evening sun had set 27 Maoists and Maoist supporters lay dead in the paddy fields and back alleys of Gaur. 15 other Maoists had been killed in nearby villages.. Almost all of them died, according to the forensic reports, from blows to

the head". This boiling over of rage had a bloody and deeply disturbing conclusion.

The day was getting late and a large amount of flies filled the red sky. The heat had dipped ever so slightly but it was still warm. I could still see animals plying the road and every so often I had to swerve to avoid colliding with a cow basking in the middle of the road. I finally reached the junction for Rajbiraj, I turned right and started to leave the highway, grateful as dusk had arrived some time ago. My limbs had started to ache a long time ago, and my backside was definitely sore, as is my throat from the dust churned up from the road.

I pulled into Rajbiraj, the district headquarters of Saptari. Some of the houses and buildings were beautiful old houses with elaborate concrete facades. But most of the charm of the town was undone by its scruffiness. The busy streets were filled with a mixture of pigs, goats, dogs, rubbish and sludge oozing from the gutters. The streets were wide, reminding me this was after all Nepal's first planned city, although not a lot appeared to have been planned. The evening heat burned down making the smell intense. I parked my bike, call my friend Pramod and we met up.

I went to his house, or rather his room. His family had a room in a shared house. There was one communal kitchen and bathroom on each floor, with a communal centre in the middle to wash clothes and this was repeated again on the second floor. The rooms were small and basic, dominated by double beds, and mats on the floor for the children to sleep on. His wife entered, she was shy and didn't speak, nor replies when I asked her name and blushes before walking away. She soon came back with tea. We sat on the bed with Pradip, Pramod's oldest son and Kumar, his nine-month-old baby. He said he had a room for me, it was next door, but when he showed me I saw that there was a small shrine on the side of the floor. Not only do I embarrassingly have a whole room to myself, when they are normally shared by families of five or more, but I'm also sleeping in the puja kota. I placed my bags down and examined my surroundings. The patchy wall had one poster, a cheap tacky photo-shopped picture of a waterfall, the type seen in barbers all over South Asia with a slogan tagged to the bottom. *"Without friends, you have nothing"*. Quite right I thought, lying down on the bed. Then on the ceiling, I saw a small green gecko several inches long protruding from a small hole. I didn't have nothing after all.

Later I left my room and saw an old man in the courtyard in a lungi working on his bicycle, he was I was told later a rickshaw wallah. He looked at me with surprise, but not the bewilderment I had expected. Few foreigners came to Saptari, and it had to be said there was no reason for them too. There was no border crossing or particularly unique points of interest. Most who do come inevitably come to talk development or politics. Saptari's main attraction seemed to be how often and excited people were to talk politics, in contrast with other places. Perhaps because it felt like there was more at stake.

Over the next few days, I tried to learn a smattering of the local dialect Maithili, which sounded like a mix of Nepali and Hindi. Yet the pronunciation is fiendishly difficult and I don't progress nearly as far as I would hope. The region is home to a plethora of languages and dialects. This is a hangover from the regions fascinating linguistic history. The Madhesh speak an Indo-Aryan dialect which arrived following migration down the Ganges valley in roughly the second millennium BC. Now, according to Whelpton

"the Terai forms a dialect continuum with speech changing gradually from one village to the next and no sharp divisions between one language and another."

Today three distinctive dialects remain and reflect these gradual geographical changes and morphing; Awadhi, Bhojpuri and Maithili. Unfortunately knowing the origins of Maithili didn't make it any easier to learn.

I was working and assisting on an ODF campaign in the district, that was what had ostensibly brought me to Saptari. This primarily involved walking around villages early in the morning checking whether homes had toilets or not. If they didn't, the community health workers would ask why not and reiterate the importance of having one. Yet this would have been much more pleasant had it not been for the police escort we were required to have, and the aggression, from both sides, in the exchanges. A huge amount of public health issues were related to open defecation and a number of schemes have been much lauded in the past but the problem remained. We walked around Norghu village and its surrounding area. We were now less than a kilometre from the border with Bihar. The number of vehicles with the BR number plate almost equalled or outnumbered the number of Nepali plated vehicles.

The villages were dusty, full of small winding lanes and were typical of any small Terai villages over Nepal, or all over the plains for that matter. Animals were the primary inhabitants of the village, with it being easy to assess the relative wealth of a household by the number of cows, bullocks and goats they had. It was normally around six or seven in the morning when we started walking around. At this time of day women de-husked rice and cut vegetables, children ran around taking the long route to school. Some older women sat around and looked after their grandchildren and older men invariably sat around on porches drinking tea in murmured conversation. Walking around the villages, all the women were decorated with elaborate tattoos on their arms and chests. More surprisingly some of the older women simply let their breasts almost hanging out on display.

We went to Pramods' mother in law's house for breakfast. I had noticed a number of birdhouses standing outside houses, complete with pigeons. They were not as it turned out, kept as a hobby or indeed for racing, rather they were a source of cheap meat. It was 9.30 in the morning and we sat outside on the caked earth floor when

Photo 17: The market in Rajbiraj

we were brought over two huge amounts of rice and small bowls of oily pigeon meat. The meat is surprisingly tender and slightly gamey, but I hope cleaner than the street pigeons from the UK. The meal is accompanied by a large helping of mango pickle, pickle so I was told, is a requisite of every Maithili meal. It was a highlight of their cuisine. This was slightly problematic as pickle was the one aspect of Nepali, or in this case Maithili, food that I had never developed a taste for. Yet here flanked by 10 people all watching my progress eating their food, I could scarcely afford to be picky and swallowed it all down. Mercifully we were able to wash it down with some brackish well water and soon allowed to walk it off.

Later that evening after work, I wandered around Rajbiraj. Some of the wide streets were flanked by beautiful old high ceilinged buildings, other buildings were decorated with old cinema posters. It was impossible to escape the fact that the city was filthy. What charm

Saptari may have was forced to compete for attention in a losing battle with the sheer filth out on the road. I saw an old cinema hall in the distance, a carved stone on its roof said it was built over 60 years ago, but I decided a closer inspection was not worth walking through the barrier of filth surrounding the building. Cows, pigs and goats all made their home here, and as a result, the smell was thick and cloying. I walked around the vegetable market, it was thronged with people and the produce on display all fresh and bountiful. Again a cacophony of sights and smells was on display, oil vendors lined up next to each other as fat men resting upon their haunches shouted out '20 rupees a kilo of aloo' or '30 rupees a kilo of cauliflower'. The market was located around a temple, built, or rather half built by Indian pilgrims. Today the top was either crumbling or an unfinished façade. I couldn't tell. The bottom floor, equally poorly constructed had been given over to shop fronts.

I meet an old school teacher, he stopped me in the street.

'Oh hello, where are you from sir?' He asked in impeccable English.

'I'm from Manchester', I replied, giving my actual hometown would be far too confusing.

'Ah the old industry city', he replied before launching into a rather detailed description of the cotton factories and industrial might of northern England in the 1800s. I was impressed. I felt he was old enough for his education to come from old colonial school books from over the border. Surely that would be the only explanation for someone thousands of miles away from being taught about the industrial history of England. That had been dry enough for me at school, let alone how dry it would be to learn with little to no context or relatability. After a few minutes pleasant conversation he walked off, he had to hurry over to an evening English class he tells me. A class he started teaching ever since retirement. I saw him walk off, dressed in an impeccably clean kurta and walk with his back straight and head held high.

Photo 18: Neta chowk in Rajbiraj

That evening Saptari seemed calm. People are mostly returning home for the evening with their vegetables, most appear more concerned with their upcoming dinner than the upcoming elections. Today there were none of the large-scale demonstrations or protests that I had seen in newspapers and on television. Yet it would be wrong to paint an image of serenity and harmony down in Saptari. There is a clear and palpable anger lying under the surface, it is not just to do with political identity. The Madhesh has some of the poorest education records for districts in Nepal. Walking around villages the under-development is clear with less than 50% of houses having toilets.

The streets have one noticeable difference from other parts of the Terai, with Saptari home to a sizable Muslim minority, potentially one of the highest in Nepal. Madrasas and mosques had broken up the monotony of mandirs on my drive down. Up to 15% of the

Madheshi population are Sunni Muslims. Many claim far-off ancestry, from Persia, Arabia and Afghanistan. But these Nepalese are highly likely to have resided here for generations.

The political scene in the Madhesh somehow manages to be even more complicated and fractured than the rest of Nepalese politics, itself already a confusing mismatch of competing warring and occasionally allying factions with intensely confusing series of acronyms. One of the most powerful elements in local politics here was the UDMF. The UDMF, or United Democratic Madhesi Front, is made of up three Madhesi political parties, the Sadbhavana Party (SP), the Terai-Madhesh Loktantrik Party (TMLP) and the Madhesh Jana Adhikhar Forum, Nepal (MJF). Yet as party leaders enjoy big personalities, acrimonious splits of political forces were all too common. Politics in the region was explosive, dangerous and almost unintelligible to outsiders, which I felt served both the government and the political parties themselves. This was not a political problem calling for outside interference.

For many outsiders, which includes people from Kathmandu and the hills of Nepal, the Madhesh is a curiosity that only becomes an issue that really needs resolving during strikes and when the Country's supply of petrol is disrupted by blockades and burning tyres. When the tyres go away and the petrol supply to Kathmandu resumes, so to go away the concerns about the Madhesh. One reason behind this apathy is undoubtedly racial, with hearing eye rising remarks about Madheshis casually made by supposedly enlightened members of Kathmandu's elite all too common. This issue was not a problem for the civil society of intelligentsia of Kathmandu to dwell on, let alone find a solution for. It was an Indian problem, as they were all Indian, or paid for by India and who would want to dirty their hands in the murky world of Indian politics. Even the token scholars of the Maoist movement had little to say

What definitely complicates political matters in Kathmandu was the undeniably and age-old link between Nepal's Terai and Northern

India. They share a roti-beti ka rishta, roti stands for bread and beti for daughters, they are considered close enough to eat the same bread and marry each other's daughters. In other words a deep relationship. This claim was reiterated in 2016 by Nepal's ambassador to India, Deep Kumar Upadhyay. There is no other country that shares the similar linguistic, religious and even in parts dietary heritage of southern Nepal as India. This roti-beti ka rishta signifies deep and longstanding ties of food and family.

For too many in Kathmandu, their interactions with Madheshis were fleeting and ultimately ephemeral. Handing bottles and old newspapers through the gate to a so-called dhoti or buying vegetables from a bhaiya, this was the limit of most people's exposure to the Madheshi. A thickly accented Nepali gave their origins away, but a darker skin colour often did that first. I had heard a few answers to the Madhesh problem in Kathmandu, none satisfactory. Developments in the Madhesh, when considered at all, were seen as a problem removed from our lives, not connected to them. It could as well be in Gujarat, Kerala or the North West frontiers of Pakistan. Onlookers from the hills often had the disinterred gaze of someone half-heartedly staring at the soles of their feet. It is impossible to argue against the fact that fears over citizenship and the fear of the other continues to colour much of the discourse surrounding the Madhesh.

For Nepal's leaders, not legitimising or giving credence to the concerns of the Madhesh is a major issue. If it becomes an area of acknowledged political concern then people are worried it would give India a potential avenue to control and influence Nepal's politics, due to its alleged affinity with Madheshis. Which is ironic because if India was indeed controlling and manipulating Nepal's politics, its method would be indeed through civil unrest and provoking political instability. Actively incorporating and including the Madhesh in a Nepali state would remove that chink in the armour for India to exploit. But in Nepal, with the Sikkimese ascension to India in 1975

Photo 19: Evening streets of Saptari

never far from people's minds, fears of foreigners controlling politics is not a fear that is likely to fade any time soon, which makes the government extending a citizenship based olive branch to the Madhesh an unlikely reality.

That evening I meet a friend, Baburam Yadav, and he insists that I stay at his house and as Pramod wanted his room back I had no real alternative and accepted. He tells me his house is just 2 kilometres out of Rajbiraj, but just after I have agreed it quickly becomes 10km. He collected me from town in the evening and to take me to his house. First, however, we go to drink. Leaving Rajbiraj behind us we rode on unilluminated roads passing paddy fields in the oncoming dark. Most the fields were not cultivated, just, in fact, left barren, often due to a lack of money or resources for water pumps or similar tools. We stopped at a wooden hut on the side of the road. Three people were outside, it was hard to mark them out in the gloom but they looked like teenagers. At that moment a police van pulled up and two men jumped out the back. It was by now past nine o clock.

'Go home you have to shut for the night' they shouted down as they walked around. Two more people straggled out of the hut clutching motorbike helmets as if to leave. 'It's done, its shut. It's past 9 pm and this shop has to shut at 9 pm', the police continued to cry out. After another minute the police, now looking satisfied moved on. We did not.

No-one had actually left, just walked into the darkness only to re-emerge when the police had left. After two minutes of idle chit-chat, the now boarded up shop removed its barricades and kept its outside light turned off before the shopkeeper ushered us inside, and locked the door behind us. The shack was small and turns out to be just a liquor shop with two benches. An old man, around fifty sat on a chair barely paying attention to a small TV under the counter blaring an Indian Premier League cricket match. He passed me a beer and waved me under a small opening where the hut opened out at the back to one of the benches. On the bench were the people from before. They were indeed teenagers. And they were drunk. With nowhere else to sit I and Baburam joined them. Immediately they start to peer over and attempted to join our conservation. They had just finished their plus 2 and one had lived in Kathmandu for 2 months.

'Do you know Deepak Kumar Jha?' asked the one who'd lived in Kathmandu.

I shook my head.

'But he lives in Balaju?'

I shook my head again.

'He works in a mobile shop in New Road'

I shook my head. At this stage, he pulled up a picture of him on his phone before shoving it in my face. I still didn't know him, I insisted. The boy looked upset

'Aah, so you don't know him?' He asks forlornly, one last time

I didn't. Naturally.

After an hour or so of drinking, us only two beers, whereas they had knocked back at an alarming rate two small 180ml bottles of whisky and two packets of cigarettes. One pulled out something sharp and shiny from his pockets and started spinning it behind his fingers.

'What's that for?' I asked, pointing at his knuckle duster, knowing full well what it was. He laughed and looked at the floor for a split second before handing me the duster. It was weighty, with an inch extension and worryingly it wasn't brand new and I wasn't sure if I wanted to know how it got so badly scuffed.

An hour later after enduring fragmented conversation, they wanted to practise their English. I finished my beer. With difficulty, I refused Baburam's requests for another one and settled the bill. With Babauram stumbling out of the bar we got on his bike. He initially struggled to kick start it, his legs were swaying slightly. Eventually, he got the bike started and we rode home to his house. It was now almost 11.

Baburam's house was a small farmer's house in a village made up of 6 other households. A small river ran behind it, slimy and dirty but the village was surrounded by paddies. The path to his house took us through the unlit village, past buffaloes, cows and goats. We entered his house and I met his wife, mother and two children who were still wide awake. Again we sat outside and were soon brought rice and chicken by Baburam's mother. Despite this being the third overly large serving of masu bhat I've eaten today I had to force it down. They passed me water, it tasted brackish and dirty.

That night, I slept in a spare room without a mosquito net, I didn't need one, Baburam assured me. It's in the other room he explained, and besides, I didn't need it this time of year. I turned the light off and climbed into bed.

I lay awake most of the night sweating and being bitten. The house was close to a temple and the overnight broadcast mantras and music did its fair share in keeping me awake that night. The mosquito bites along long with the heat did the rest.

The next day my knees and arms were a putrid shade of dark red and purple from the hundreds of bites I'd suffered the night before. Looking down I saw that my t-shirt and shorts were dotted with small spots of dried blood. More urgently, however, last night's chicken or pigeon had not agreed with me. I got out of bed and walked over to the outhouse. Returning, I walked past the house and down the pitted road to the edge of a paddy. Before me, the early morning mist hung heavy. In the distance, I could see buffalos and a lone women already working in the fields. The trees in the distance were obscured by cloud, it was damp and for the only time of the day, almost chilly. I walked back, disturbing a couple of sleeping goats on my return back to the house. After tea, I headed back to Rajbiraj.

The next few days passed in a blur of heat, dust, villages and snatched sleep in sweltering heat.

The Eastern Hills

Ilam

After finishing things up in Saptari I had hoped to continue my trip to Ilam and Hile on my Honda. But by now the bike was starting to fall apart. Three years of constant abuse had taken its toll. It never really recovered from repeatedly being dragged around dirt roads in rural Nepal, particularly after the earthquake. I was fast losing confidence in its ability to survive one more slog through the hills. I had some work to attend to in Kathmandu and needed to get my bike seen to, but I resolved to return to eastern Nepal as soon as possible just without the liability of an unreliable motorbike.

A week later I bought a ticket on a night bus to Ilam. I had sat the night before in my room preparing for the trip as if it was any other. Selecting reading materials, maps and clothes. Yet this time it would not just be a normal trip. It would be my final one in Nepal. Or at least the final one for some time. Three weeks after I left on my bus to the eastern hills I would be going on another journey. Only this time it would involve a Thai Airways flight to Bangkok. I had taken a job in a human rights organisation in northern Thailand and would be leaving Nepal for the considerable future. While I would come back, it wouldn't be the same. I had arrived into Nepal 3 years ago on a flight from Istanbul. I spent three listless days in Istanbul before arriving in Kathmandu, I had been impatient to arrive and numb to the Byzantine ruins as I counted down the hours until my new life in Nepal began. Yet now, my master's course, the ostensible reason for my spending 3 years in Kathmandu, was finally over. I was moving on. A lot had happened in those three years. I had completed a master's degree, travelled the length of the country, had a series of strange and varied employment experiences and learned a language. My time in Nepal had a constant sense of malaise. The constant pull of having to be in class six evenings a week, and working predominately early in the morning had meant I had an inordinate amount of time at my disposal. A large quantity of it I frittered away, but some were spent wandering Kathmandu's streets at night, getting lost on motorbikes, learning Nepali and most of all reading a considerable amount of books. Whatever I could find in Kathmandu's small collection of second-hand bookshops. I had now left my studies behind, and whilst eager and excited to move on, was slightly sad and melancholic for the life I would be leaving behind. Often it had been a Kafkaesque combination of elation and depression, yet always enriching.

Ilam was a place that I had heard a lot about, but only in fragments. It was the reputed home of the tea gardens of Nepal, but it existed in the shadow of its noisier, better-heeled and considerably wealthier eastern Neighbour. Darjeeling was after all just a stone's throw away. Ilam boasted the same climate, topography and geographic features of its richer cousin, but with a fraction of the tourists. I had felt Darjeeling to be underwhelming and a bit of a facade. Hotels remained called the Windermere and the Elgin were quaint enough on paper, but today's pretence seems slightly sad and almost comical in the flesh. People were clinging onto a history that had long gone. Only remnants and fragments of memory and history were left. No longer held shackled to the image of an English village in the hills, Darjeeling should rediscover itself with a new image, not like some poorly kept relic of the colonial times stuffed with Anglo-Indian caricatures, but what it is and what it always was. A bustling bazaar town. When the well-to-do sahibs and memsahibs descended en masse to the hill station they had been descending into an illusion, albeit one that had been in everyone's best interests to maintain. Now, Darjeeling was a mass of concrete, shop fronts and buses, home to people from all over north-eastern India, all over the plains and Nepal. The sheer number of people and scale of buildings held the eye rather than the 18th-century Anglican churches. To see people from Darjeeling cling to a historical fallacy long after any remnants have left is bewildering when unconsidered and then deeply sad afterwards. Darjeeling could not make its mind up of what it was it a historical relic to be preserved, or an important bazar town boasting one of the most important education centers for eastern India. The sahibs had been replaced by vacationing Indians. The eclectic collection of Anglo-Indians who firmly clung onto the British ways long after 1947 seemed so wretchedly pathetic at times, sporting overstressed accents and complaining about things not being the same since 1947 despite the fact most of them had been born long after independence.

Ilam, with no colonial fabrications to cover and distort its image, seemed a rather attractive and a fitting way to round of my time in Nepal. After my trip to Darchula earlier on in the year this would be, albeit with a three-month gap in Kathmandu, my own Mahakali to Mecchi. From Ilam, I had hoped to stop off at Hile, Dharan and Biratnagar on my way back and to make a final call in Saptari, before heading back to Kathmandu for the last time.

At 4 pm on a Tuesday I arrived at Gongabu, full as ever with all the typical sights, smells and activity of any transport hub in South Asia. Students hung around waiting for buses to take them home after exams. Men working in Kathmandu eagerly waited to return home for the first time in months. Grandparents were arriving to visit family working in the city. In many ways, Gongabu had more energy and suspense and bustle and was a more emotionally charged place than Tribhuvan International Airport. I would argue for the vast majority of Nepalese, it was more important. While domestic air flight had made large inroads in the last few years, it was still predominately the preserve of the wealthy. Advancements in aviation aside, there were still many places in Nepal where the only access was by road. Buses and jeeps play and will continue to hold a vitally important role in the lives of millions of Nepalese.

Just before I got out of my taxi it started to rain, but not just rain. The pre-monsoon rains had been threatening to break for the last few days, and now they broke. I walked over to the bus rank as the rain lashed down, creating a cacophony of sounds, the rain reverting of the metal buses of the roofs and the tin roofs of buildings. Already drenched I found my bus five minutes before departure time. Half an hour later, however, there was still no sign of the driver. I sat in my seat watching people huddle under shop awnings in desperate attempts to stay dry, while many of the young boys working as assistants on the bus instead trudged futilely through the rain. Finally with the driver showing up forty minutes after our scheduled departure time the old bus, deluxe in name only, crawled out of the bus park to join the rush hour traffic.

I had last headed to the east via Dhulikhel and the BP Koirala highway. Less than a week ago I had gone and returned on that highway, unfortunately, while the diverted road was fine for bikes and smaller microbuses it wasn't suitable for the larger buses. We, therefore, would have to take the Prithvi Highway to Mugling instead. With the state of the diverted road over the BP Koirala highway, and the amount of rain that would be cloying up and weighing the earth down, it probably made sense, but heading west for several hours, before dropping down at Mugling was hardly the route that I would have chosen. None the less, we rolled out of Kalanki and around an hour later, leaving the commuting traffic behind, we dropped down to Naubise and I left the Kathmandu Valley for the last time.

It was not long now until the sun started to set. We made our way down to the crude rough road to Nararyanghat and the East-West Highway. It was now almost dark, the rain has slowed but it was still drizzling, I got my head down and tried to get some rest while the bus slowly bumped along its way to Ilam.

When I awoke, dawn was breaking. I was greeted with the now familiar sights of Lahan and realised we had come nowhere near as far expected. We were supposed to reach Ilam by around 8, it was now 6. Passing through Lahan and then Saptari I was able to stretch out and take in the surroundings, the one luxury offered by a bus as opposed to the bike. Dawn was now breaking along the banks and tributaries of the Koshi River.

Again I noticed how in the majority of the paddies which were being cultivated were relatively small and lay close to the road. On closer inspection, they were clearly for household consumption. Swathes of barren land behind the paddies went unused and just lay there in the dust. With this, I closed my eyes again and tried to sleep but was continually rocked awake. I sat, half awake, watching the morning dew and haze lift from the Terai and I let the plains roll into and become one monotonous blur only broken by the odd roadside settlement, bullock cart, small tempo or the structure of a funeral pyre by a ghat near a dried out riverbed. We passed the entrance to the Koshi Tappu Wildlife Reserve, one of the smaller wildlife reserves in Nepal and famous for its density of different species of birds.

Not long later we arrived at the Koshi barrage. The Koshi barrage followed the Koshi agreement of 1954 and it remained a contentious issue today, one that brought on anger and shame to many Nepalis. A dam would be constructed to block the Koshi River, one of the largest rivers in Nepal, and a river that when it floods can cause havoc to millions in Bihar. But the dam would be built by India and Nepal would contentiously only receive its share based upon its current capacity at the time of construction, as opposed to in line with future expansion. India would also share control of the damn with Nepal. This damn became the current Koshi barrage. The bus rolled over the barrage. Although the backwaters were sleepy, by the barrage the roadside was busy and bustling. Men lined the side of the road with this morning's catch, some have small fish, while others sell significantly bigger fish, possibly from Janakapur. Looking towards my right, on the other side of the dam boats plied the waterfront, complete with nets drawled over the side of boats. We trundle along over the barrage to the other side of the river and as the sun broke we were well on our way to Ithari.

As we finally entered Morang and Jhapa the scenery was noticeably different from Saptari and Lahan, the dust had been replaced with grass, and the scrubland replaced with forests. Houses were built on stilts, with grazing area below for animals and were vastly different from before. The shops and houses that lined the roads looked more affluent and better constructed and there is, as we approach Ithari, a wealth of electrical shops and car and bike dealerships are situated along the road. The eastern Terai is well documented to be richer and more developed than the western part, and that was immediately clear. But it is not just the wealth of the towns that contrasted with the Saptari and Lahan, the ethnic makeup of the towns is much more mixed between people from the hills and people from the plains. We continued, flanked by sparse forest on one side and houses on the other. Soon I saw, on the right-hand side of the road, the unmistakable outline and silhouette of tea plants. I had finally arrived in the land of Nepal's tea plantations. The area was now lush and green, and cultivatable. Perhaps the biggest diff erence was the absence of grit in my teeth. Here I saw fertile plains, gardens with an oasis of mango and fruit trees. The smell of animal fertiliser, for the first time, fills the bus as does the unmistakable smells of farms, cattle and livestock. Saptari had similar sights, but the dust does its best to mask any semblance of smell or fragrance and hides its rich agricultural potential. The soil here does not look tired or in its death throes.

The Siwalik hills, which hugged my left and what had been a constant companion in my journey along the highway dip in and out of focus. The early morning haze robs them of their clarity, but now we are reaching Birtamode. We passed through it, another town built around the highway. Finally, as Biratmode becomes a blur behind us we reach the junction for the Mechi Highway and the road to Ilam. As the bus slowed down but didn't stop, the bus assistant stuck his head out of the door looking for jeeps to Ilam. A jeep near a chowk was filling up, and the bus slowed more to let me jump off. As the bus accelerated away to Kakavitta and the Indian border, I wandered over to the jeep.

It was a small Tata Sumo, with seats for around eight, but already there are about twelve people squashed inside. I took a seat on the parcel shelf in the boot. Yet I was not alone, there were five chicken hatchlings squawking and residing in an upturned bowl, but worryingly three further seats in the boot. They soon get filled and all squashed together we pull off. It was now 10 am, and the heat from the sun was intense in mid-May and I was eager to leave the plains behind and start to ascend towards the cooler air of the hills

We pulled left from the highway and headed in a straight line towards the Siwalik hills. Away from the highway, it was noticeably greener and even lusher than before, and now our journey was flanked by tea gardens. It immediately reminded me of the fertile lower hills of West Bengal, unsurprisingly, after all, they were so close.

On the drive, it was not long before we passed through Kanyam. This was cruelly deceptive, the road cut through almost impossibly idyllic tea gardens and small rolling hills stretching long past the horizon in picture-perfect unbroken undulating fields of green shrubbery. I felt as if Ilam was only around the corner. Then I saw a sign saying Ilam, 44km. Soon the rows of tea finished and we were back in the cover of the forest and I don't see any tea gardens until we entered the outskirts of Ilam over two hours later.

The journey to Ilam was supposed to take three hours; it took us almost five. It turns out I wasn't the only one concerned with the jeep being overloaded. As, inevitably, we had picked up roadside stragglers the overcrowded jeep now had two guys hanging off the back, which actually isn't as uncomfortable as it looks, and while concentration is required you do avoid the nails, screws and metal runners that so often dig into your back when you get a seat. For the first hour or so, the two guys, the youngest often seem to get designated hanging off the back status, had been diving into the boot out of sight whenever we passed a police check post.

With the outskirts of the town in the distance we pulled up one hundred metres before a particularly large checkpoint, the driver shouted at the two men to jump off and walk behind and not look like they know anyone. We left them walking on the road and pulled up at the checkpoint. After the customary blue book and license check, the policeman asked how many people were travelling in the jeep. Only 15 says the driver, but the policeman looks unconvinced. He strolled around the jeep, lingered around and didn't wave us away just yet. Sure enough, ten seconds later the two guys strolled past the jeep. Yet their attempt to look as if they have been hiking doesn't pass muster. One, the youngest, had spotless white jeans on, the other is rotund and hadn't broken a sweat, despite seemingly having climbed kilometres from the plains. What was worse the younger one looked at the jeep and winked. The policeman noticed it, and feeling vindicated, promptly issued a ticket to the driver for driving with more than 15 passengers, still considerably more than is safe, and sent the boys on their way. Naturally around the first corner past the checkpoint, we waited and the two guys clambered again onto the back of the bus before we continued to Ilam. Then we got a puncture.

I read in a brochure one story of the origin of the name Ilam was that it was derived from the Limbu phrase meaning tortuous road, whether that was true or not seemed almost redundant, it was a good story and rather apt. I quickly made my mind up to avoid any other origin story that could poke a hole in this fitting anecdote.

Ilam and what now constitutes modern-day Nepal was added to the expanding Gorkha Empire in September 1774 and taken from the Kirat Chiefs and the Kirat Pradesh. One reason for this expansion was a desire to control the expansive and lucrative Tibetan trade. By controlling the passes to Tibet, they would be able to monopolise the trade. A treaty signed in 1775 with Tibet solidified these desires by stipulating all Tibetan trade routes would only pass through Nepal on their journey south. When in 1784 trade was opened by Tibet through the Chumbi valley, which leads through Sikkim, Nepal shut down this loophole by invading and conquering Sikkim in 1788. The invasion moved from Ilam, through Darjeeling and into Chyakhung in Sikkim.

This aggressive outward expansion under the Gorkha empire, continuing the almost manifest destiny approach of Prithvi Narayan Shah has been since described as nation-building, and one of Prithvi's biggest, if not greatest achievement. But, at the time, there was little national identity extending out of the Kathmandu Valley, itself is known to many as Nepal. It would certainly be news to an 18th Century Magar in Dolpa, or Kirati in Taplejung that they were in fact, Nepalese and living in a country called Nepal. This is reinforced by some of the first lines of Francis Buchanan Hamilton in his Account of the Kingdom of Nepal and of the Territories Annexed to this Dominion by the House Gorkha. Writing in the early 1800s, an Account of the Kingdom before its war with the British in 1814, Buchanan opened with the words

"Nepal, a name celebrated in Hindu legend, in a strict sense, ought to be applied to that country only which is in the vicinity of Kathmandu, the capital but at present, it is usually given to the whole territory of the Gorkha Rajas"

He later uses the term 'Nepal Proper' to describe areas in the mid-hills extending from Kathmandu. Further, in living memory, according to Kumar Pradhan in 1968 researchers and tourists observed that in some mountain tribes and villages the inhabitants were *"not aware that the Nation of Nepal exists"*. This Greater Nepal was unified by conquest but hardly by feelings of kinship. Assorted rebellions were common until the Suguali treaty of 1816 significantly shrank the borders of Nepal.

Finally around nineteen long hours after leaving Kathmandu I arrived in Ilam. The bazaar was smaller than I imagined and pleasantly quiet. The streets were small, one car width, but not busy enough to feel congested. I wandered around the bazaar and strolled through the gardens and out of town. There were some beautiful bungalows set aside from the bazaar with rolling views of the tea plantations.

Unlike its better known foreign neighbour, Ilam was not full of overpriced hotels and expensive gift packets of tea. I wandered up to my hotel outside of the bazaar and climbed the nearby view tower. Now in mid-May, the pre-monsoon haze had set in and things were not as clear as they should be. The tea gardens gave a soft edge to the view. They almost smoothed out the otherwise aggressive outline of Nepal's hills as seen in so many places elsewhere in the country. The plant coverage and plantation was far from uniform, in areas the rows of tea plants are straight as a ruler, in others, they are placed at seemingly random intervals and without design or structure.

Yet, like all tea gardens, there was little to do apart from to wander around the shrubbery. I did just that. I noticed while walking around, the overwhelming majority of tourists are domestic honeymooners. The few foreign tourists have all come from Darjeeling. There is none of the colonial stiffness or stuffiness associated with so many South Asian tea plantations. Be it Darjeeling, just over the border, or Nuwara Eliya in Sri Lanka, these places have seemed to suffer from an identity crisis. In the 21st century, what purpose does a colonial

Photo 20: The Tea Gardens of Ilam

hill station entertain? Ilam seemed, by contrast, positively confident in its identity. Soon after I returned to my hotel, I pulled up a chair outside overlooking the tea gardens and congenially spent an evening drinking beer and reading about the lost Gurkha Kingdom.

The next day I wandered lackadaisically on a long walk through the gardens. I wandered further and further from the town, on a small path snaking away from the bazaar. The morning mist had been replaced by a thick haze blown theatrically over and around the bushes. The air was complete with morning birdsong only broken occasionally by the shouts of little children, some who by my reckoning now must be seriously late for school.

After two hours I arrived on the main road several kilometres down from the bazaar and started walking back up. Even the bazaar, when I return was relaxed and quiet. Here a good two out of three shops were closed for the day and apart from the few jeeps plying people up and down the Mechhi highway, all was quiet. Ilam had the feel of a quiet sleepy backwater, despite its role as a major employer in the region. It was unsurprising then, when I ask people what to do, or what to see, many simply told me to spend my time relaxing.

As I was wandering through the bazaar, trying unsuccessfully it seems to find a barber that were open, I heard a cry across the chowk 'Bhai!' I stopped in my tracks and looked around, at this time of day with all the early morning jeeps and buses having left, the small bus park was full of old men having tea. I saw a man, sitting on a table around 20 metres away gesturing towards me. I pointed to myself and he nodded. I walked over and sat down on the chair offered. The man was in his forties with the ubiquitous paunch that was so common in many middle-aged men. He was dressed in an old, but expensive looking sports jacket and had a flashy watch on his wrist. He introduced himself in halting English as Devi, I replied in Nepali. He was, as he told me the president of the local Ilam Hotel Association and had a whole list of questions for me, with nothing else pressing to do, I settled in for a long discussion.

'So how long will you be staying in Ilam for?' he asked

'Just a few days' I replied, preparing for the inevitable reply

'Oh my God, such a short time!'

'I know' I replied, trying to look as glum as possible.

He talked about the area and gave a great sales pitch.

Ilam, so I was quickly told, is famous for seven products that begin with the 'aa' consonant in the Nepali language. These are, he tells me beaming with obvious pride, aalaichi, or cardamom, aduwa, ginger, aalu, potato, amlisho, a material used to make a broom aaolan, milk, aakabare khorsani, round chillies and finally arthodox tea, so close to orthodox tea but sounded to me like a convenient misspelling.

He went onto ask how he can get more volunteers to the area. There may be a lot in other parts of the country, but comparatively few here in Ilam. As I started to offer up an explanation, the man seated to his left, an older Kirati gentleman with paan-stained teeth interrupted.

'Where in the UK are you from?'

'Manchester,'

'Ah, my family are living in the UK. My mother, brother, father all are in the UK'

'Are they in Aldershot?' I asked and he nodded in reply. Aldershot has the largest population of Nepalese residing in the UK, as Aldershot is a barracks of the Gurkha brigade, the overwhelming majority are former Gurkhas and their families. Lots of eastern Nepalese have joined the Gurkhas and a combination of remittance and opportunities for foreign education has been a massive boom to the area and has undoubtedly contributed towards the affluence of this region. His father, the man continues, served in the Falklands and his grandfather served in WW2, in the Burma campaign of 1941. He was clearly very proud of his heritage, and several of the other men who had gathered also had family members in the UK who served in the Gurkhas and retired in or near Aldershot. The talk turns to the UK and the Gurkhas. When I complain about their lack of benefits and that they are underpaid I was rewarded with some sympathetic nods.

From their first real encounter, the British were struck by the bravery and commitment of the Gurkha troops they faced. Byron Farwell writes in a history of the Gorkhas, *"the British admiration for their Nepalese enemies had been such that they could hardly wait for the war to end before enlisting Gurkhas into their own battalion".*

After signing the Suguali treaty following defeat in the Gurkha Wars of 1814-16, Nepal had several repercussions. They had to give away large tracts of land, submit to a permanent British resident and not to allow foreigners employment in Nepal, apart from the British of course. There was also a section of the Suguali treaty which stated that Gurkhas,

"will be at liberty to enter into the service of the British government, if agreeable to themselves and the British government accept their service".

On 24 April 1815, the first Gurkha battalion was formed in Sirmoor, the Simoor Rifles. The Battalion had been through several changes and amalgamations and it is now known today as the Royal Gurkha Rifles. Ever since 1815 Nepalese have been recruited into regiments all over the world, most famously in the UK, but also in India, Brunei, and Singapore

The Gurkhas stood to get a pay much higher than available in Nepal, an education and also pride. The British gained strong, reliable troops, and most conveniently a cheap supply of troops. One more strategic reason behind the Gorkha recruitment in the 1830s was to weaken the strength of, and therefore the threat from, the Nepalese military. Brian Hodgson, the famed resident of Nepal pushed heavily for Gurkha recruitment. I had found, in a report on the catalogue of the Hodgson collection by John Whelpton and Michael Hutt in an old copy of the European Bulletin of Himalayan Research, a lucid account of what the representatives of the East India Company felt about the strategic benefits of Gurkha recruitment. The account found that Hodsgon held *"strong conviction that Nepal's continuing resentment of the loss of a third of its territory after the 1814-16 war, its isolationist policies and its maintenance of a large standing army were a continuing threat to peace and this should be removed by encouraging the growth of commerce and by employing the country's' surplus military manpower' in the East India Company's forces"*

The conversation now turned back to me and my trip. Everyone, very seriously, was insisting I had made a mistake with my trip and needed to stay for longer. Trying to frown and look serious I nodded in agreement and apologised for my heinous mistake. The group soon opened for questions and soon I appeared to be holding court, answering questions that were now past familiar. I could answer these questions in my sleep, they have now become repeated enough times to almost become scripture.

'Why do you study in Nepal?'

'Where did you learn Nepali?'

'How old are you?'

'How many brothers and sisters do you have?'

'What does your father do?'

And the necessary, after I said I worked in Kathmandu, *'how much do you earn?'*

With nothing else to do I was more than happy to sit and talk until the rain clouds threatened ominously overhead and it was almost time to leave.

With loose promises to return and for me Devi and Prateek, the elder gentlemen, to share a journey to Sandakpur after the monsoon, a viewpoint by the border with Sikkim. They showed me pictures of the place, and although it looked nice I highly doubted Devi's claims we can see into Bhutan and see Mt Everest. One older man chimed in that he had seen Annapurna from Sanpakpur. Other people murmured in agreement whilst I tried to hold a straight face and nodded very seriously. After swapping numbers and showing Devi where to advertise online for tourists and volunteers, it was time to leave.

On my last evening in Ilam, it started to rain from mid-afternoon and it didn't stop for 3 hours. When it finally did the haze cleared with the rain and I was afforded with a view I have not seen before, previously obscured by the haze. I could see right down to the plains, a clear geographical barrier is evident between the plains and the hills. A river cut its way almost aggressively through the flat landscape. At least I thought it was a river, it must have been a 100km away but the afternoon sun's unmistakable glint was clear to me.

I ordered a tea, black and it came full of sugar. Despite high tea production, the majority was not for domestic consumption, certainly not the expensive first flush teas and I thought back to Devi when he told me lots of Ilam tea was often repackaged at Darjeeling tea.

I sat again later that evening outside my hotel with a beer and a book and watched the clouds get blown around by the wind in the valley below me.

Hile

The next morning at 5.30 in the morning, the jeep for Hile arrived at the gates of the hotel. We headed down to the bazaar and had tea in the bus park before we left at 6. In the khajar ghar I am soon surrounded by men asking me questions in Nepali and trying to force cigarettes in my hand. The typical questions of where am I from, what I am doing was quickly dispatched with so we could move onto the much more important questions of the morning, namely how much did I like Nepali girls? After this, one man was particularly keen to talk about Yamo Buddha, one of Nepal's most famous rappers, who died in mysterious circumstances in London last year. No, he did not commit suicide, the thirty old year iterates and reiterates, he was killed by his wife over money. This, he assures me, was a fact. Yet I would be much more inclined to believe him was he not, despite the early hour, raging drunk and struggling to stand up. Whether he was drunk from last night or this morning I could not be sure.

I sat in the front seat of the jeep with Uttam Kafle, a project manager for a local NGO and Sanjay the driver. They were both happy to talk and we discussed, politics, development, eastern Nepal and the upcoming elections. Uttam recommended me to stay in Hile but warned me away from Dhankuta. *'There is nothing to do there and the people can be a little difficult'*. But then again as there wasn't exactly a plethora of things to do in Ilam, I resolved to ignore this advice, particularly the senseless warning about the people being difficult. Then, with nothing else to do for 3 hours we made tentative plans to travel to Sandakpur, my second such plan, when he left we exchanged phone numbers, although both of us knew we wouldn't go trekking it was fine. We had the air of two old friends talking about arranging a reunion who both knew wouldn't happen.

After we arrived back down in the plains, we headed west for several kilometres before we started to climb again. Five hours after setting off in the morning, we arrived in Dharan, where Sanjay and I went for lunch. He knew a place and as it turned out most other drivers in eastern Nepal. When I try to pay for my masu bhat, he waves me hand away. *'I don't need your money'* he protested. The lunch I noticed, was not a lot cheaper than the price I'd paid for the ticket. When I walked through Dharan, he placed his arm over mine. Whether it was an act of defence from the touts nearby or merely a show of affection I wasn't sure. We exchanged phone numbers and I promised to call him next time that I had a free evening in Dharan.

Dharan is an affluent town, the British Gurkha recruitment Centre was established here in 1953 and this soon became a massive draw for recruits and their family. Returning Gurkhas often came to reside in Dharan and it was this combination of remittance, returning ex-Gurkhas and a broad ethnic mix that turned Dharan into a dynamic city. Supposedly both the capital of Nepal's fashion industry and so I'm told, the birthplace of the majority of Nepali footballers. It was cleaner than other cities, looked better planned and there were definitely some very well dressed Nepalis strutting around the bus station.

The Gurkhas are one of the most visible legacies of Nepal's and Britain's history, particularly in Dharan. While now they enjoy good relations and the UK is one of Nepal's largest bi-lateral donors it was not always this way. 200 years ago the Gurkha Kingdom and the British East India Company shared a bloody history of wars, aggression and tactics designed to be both humiliating and ruthless. The initial skirmishes were fought over territories until the situation escalated and culminated in the Gurkha Wars of 1814-16 and the eventual Suguali treaty.

The Gurkha Kingdom was a fantastically ruthless and cutthroat world, full of political deviance, alliances and betrayals, in line with other kingdoms of the time. Leading Nepal required serious political acumen, particularly to remain independent from the all engorging British East India Company to the south. The Gurkha Kingdom threw up some intricate and wonderfully intriguing characters. One was Jung Bahadur Rana. Another was Bhimsen Thapa.

Bhimsen Thapa was a young courtier who became the mukhtiyar of Nepal in a bloody coup in 1806 and reigned until 1837. At the height of Gurkha expansion, the British asked the Nepalese to leave disputed lands in the Punjab, Bhimsen agreed. Yet when presented with another demand from the British to withdraw to the east, from Butwal and Syuraj, Bhimsen refused. The Gurkha Kingdom and the East India Company were now at war.

Bhimsen Thapa may have been a master of domestic battles and manoeuvring, however, his large territories had expanded fast and required reform. However, according to Nepali Historian Baburam Acharya,

> *"Bhimsen lacked diplomatic acumen. He failed to grasp the largely deceitful political strategies of the British. While corruption was rife, the administration of unified Nepal, which now spread from the Tista in the east to beyond the Alaknanda in the west, cried out for reforms so as to bring about progress to the nation. But Bhimsen utilized most of his time and resources to augment his own power and riches as well as those of his family. The need to strengthen and make more efficient the state administration was perpetually overlooked".*

The war with the East India Company was avoidable: the controversy was over disputed areas of land. By handing over these remote areas of land, where Nepal had little presence anyway, Bhimsen could have avoided war and retained the rest of Nepal's hard-won territory. A lack of knowledge about his British enemies military combined with a steadfast determination would see the end to Greater Nepal. Despite lacking military of battlefield experience nor knowing the entry points to the Kingdom Bhimsen took a military approach to the problem. It was not to work out. A much larger East India Company army was able to defeat the Gorkhas.

The equally humiliating Suguali treaty that followed was the effective end of the continually expansionist Gorkha Kingdom, no more territory would be gained by Gorkha military mite. Yet the charismatic Bhimsen Thapa was able to ride out this immensely disappointing defeat. In fact, Bhimsen, a master of Machiavellian political cunning rode his luck and considerable political knowledge until the manifestations of the East India Company and his own political rivals led to his eventual downfall and imprisonment by Queen Samrajyalaxmi. Locked in his cell, torn up by doubts he eventually slashed his throat with his own Kukhri on 22 July 1839. By now deemed a persona non grata he was left to a very unceremonious end. His attempt to kill himself had left his throat only partially cut, yet he would be granted no quarter in death. Bhimsen's semiconscious body was dumped on the banks of the Bisnumati. There

'lashed by the mid-monsoon winds and rain Bhimsen hovered between life and death for nine days, before finally breathing his last on the river bank, on 30 July 1839, at the age of sixty-four'.

His brutal rule had been matched by an equally brutal death, in the exact same place he had left rivals and family members to be torn about by dogs, vultures and jackals at the height of his power.

After eating food I waited in the bus park in Dharan. Again I thought that bus stations in Nepal had a palpable energy, completely different from those in the UK, where long-distance buses are grey, miserable and depressing. Here is different there is colour, noise, smells and the sights of a bustling transport hub.

After half an hour of waiting in the midday sun, I got on a bus bound for Dhankuta and Hile. The road to Dhankuta and Hile rose steeply from Dharan. After thirty minutes or so the road was firmly high in the hills, and looking back we were afforded a splendid view of Dharan. I looked down through the window as the bus wound its way up and I see Dhahran nestled below at 1184ft, right at the edge of the Terai and the start of the hills. The British built road climbed and dropped down two or three valleys before arriving two hours later in Dhankuta. It was now around 3 pm and as the bus pulled into Dhankuta Bazaar I hopped off. The bus came to a halt for a cigarette and toilet break. I got a chance to catch my bearings and assessed Dhankuta. My plan had been to stay here for a day and then walk or hitch a lift to Hile. I walked around the bus station and looked around at the nearby hills. After five minutes my new plan of action was clear. The bus by now was pulling slowly out of the bazaar, I chased after it and jumped back up the steps, luckily before it had picked up sufficient speed. I meekly bought another ticket for Hile, a hill station only 13km away. Surely it had more to offer than Dhankuta. I thought back to the jeep ride from Ilam with Uttam Kafle, and his questions about why I wanted to stay in Dhankuta, and advice to go stay in Hile. I realised not for the first time, I needed to get better at taking advice. In Dhankuta apart from a small non-descript Bazaar, there was little immediately on offer.

Hile was a small, but important, non-descript Bazaar town that does not really extend far past the road that continues to Basantapur. A small Tibetan influence and 2 small Gompas are the only things that distinguishes Hile from any other Bazaar town, quite like any other I passed through on the Dhankuta road. Well, that and its unique chowk. Many towns and villages in Nepal have named chowks after important people from history. Kathmandu has named several after gods, or poets and signers, such as Narayan Gopal Chowk at the northernmost tip of the ring road. In the Madhesh they are often named after martyrs, such as in Lahan. Yet here, bucking the trend and hinting at the preferred pastime of the inhabitants of Hile, the chowk was called Tongba chowk. Tonbga is a form of hot beer made from fermented millet that you add hot water to and suck through a metal straw. The tonbga here is apparently famous. I knew what I would be drinking that night.

Supposedly there are great and mesmerising views of the Himalayas from Hile, but now after a long drive from Ilam, it was almost 4 pm and the afternoon haze had firmly set in. I found a small hotel in the bazaar and left my bags behind. Uttam had recommended me going to the Horizon Hotel for luxury. I didn't want to spend the amount required to stay there but figured it would be a nice place to go for a beer. It was a few kilometres out and up from town and I had seen it repeatedly advertised on signposts on my way up. I reached there after thirty minutes walking up on the roads from the bazaar and on arrival I got a weird feeling. If the hotel wasn't designed to funnel and hide ill-gained money, the architect should have been fired. It was weird; there was a big imposing glass structure attached to the front of the hotel. From the outside, you would imagine it offered great views all around. Except when I enter there is nothing behind the glass and its thick tinting obscures much from view. There was no-one there and the only guest is a strange atmosphere. I climbed the stairs to the top floor, expecting a restaurant with views all down the valley. There were views, but the restaurant was situated on the second floor without windows. There was a huge glass façade on the front of the hotel, but the tinting was so dark it was hard to see outside. I had hoped the half an hour walk would offer good views but they didn't, nor could I get a cold beer. When I had called up an hour ago and spoken in Nepali to enquire out of interest and see if I could wrangle a discount, the rooms then had been three thousand rupees. When I went in person now, more out of curiosity than anything else and spoke in English the price started at six thousand.

The hotel was weird, despite being high up on a ridge which offered great views, the Makalu Himalayan range was behind the hotel, out of view for guests.

I wandered back down to the bazaar, feeling very glad I hadn't lugged all my things up to the hotel, only to walk rather empty handed back down to the bazaar. I sat in a khaja ghar and ordered a tongba and watched the evening buses trundle on their way down to Dharan. A boy around 8 interrupted my thoughts while bringing over a thermos of hot water for the tongba.

'*You speak Nepali*' he asks

'*Yes*' I replied

'*English?*'

'*Yes*'

'*Hindi*'

'*No?*'

'*Ah*', he laughed in the husky and confident tone of a village child, '*I speak all three!*' I laugh taken aback and for the next twenty minutes we watched the TV together, There was an IPL match on, Delhi

Daredevils vs Kolkata Night Riders. I supported Kolkata, he supported Delhi. Over the course of the game, he chastised me for my poor Hindi and weak Nepali pronunciation. I laughed heartily. I did not miss the stuffiness of Kathmandu and realised if more expats in Nepal were aware that almost every eight years old in the country had more linguistic ability than them it may inspire them to learn more than a token smattering of the language.

Cricket, I realised as we kept watching, was a great leveller. I had never had a real interest in it and my cricket career died young. I remembered the sheer boredom of being a fielder in my local cricket team. Yet here, despite a chasm of difference, an eight-year-old and I could discuss the various merits of Virat Kohli versus Sachin Tendulkar. I felt at home and whenever I mispronounced a name, the boy would scold me before breaking out into laughter.

Later that evening I sat on my little balcony drinking warm beer and pondering. It was now too late to read, the sun had set and the light socket on my balcony was missing a bulb. Soon I would be leaving Nepal, it had been a tumultuous three years, full of ups and downs. It seemed fitting to have completed, my own form of Mahakali to Mecchi. I sat and listened to the noises and sounds below me from the bazaar. The smell of unburnt sulphur from overloaded jeeps, and the smells of peppers, fire from chulos, the plumes of smoke from the buses and the hint of mountain air all collided. I watched four young children in school uniform run down the hill on their way home, the sun was long down and school finished hours ago. As they ran, they pushed and shoved each other gaily with a childish innocence that contrasted with the child of the same age who I had just been watching TV with. Nepal was like that, a country divided. By language, history, ethnicity and politics, but more than anything by money. Children of Maoists, UML, Congress and RPP all attended the same schools and sometimes shared the same holidays. Rich Tamangs, Bahuns, Rais, Chettris and Gurungs all drank at the same places and shared the same jokes over beer, just often with different protagonists. No, the one unifying thing a poor Kirati kid working in a tea shop in the eastern Himalayas had with a poor Yadav farmer in western Nepal, or a Madheshi child labourer in a brick kiln in the outskirts of Kathmandu was the sheer lack of opportunities. In a world that liked to define its self by identity, nothing had a more powerful identity than money.

That evening I sat alone, the only guest in the Hotel Tourism, aptly, if plainly named, and while I waited for my food I get chatting to Ravi, a small 20-year-old man working at the hotel. He too, like so many here, had relatives in the UK. Their comparative opportunities and wealth compared to Ravi clearly grated and he was desperate to leave. We got talking about the Gurkhas. In the early 1990s, the former eastern Gurkha recruitment camp in Dharan closed. Previously the walk to recruitment centres would take the candidates on a journey, either a few days to a few weeks, often barefoot, before they would arrive at the recruitment centre. Still, all this and they still had to pass through the intense selection process. Many were turned away for diseases often unknown to the recruiters. Others were sent away being for underweight or too small. Now candidates from all over Nepal had to report to Pokhara. Considering Gurkhas used to be known as lahuries following the British Afghan Campaign of 1848 when recruits had to travel to the cantonment in Lahore, the present journey to Pokhara is comparatively easy although the selection process waiting for them is anything but. Their selection training involves a gruelling and frankly archaic 4.7km run up Sarangkot complete with a doko loaded with 25kg of sand. Ravi had tried twice in the past and failed both times.

'It was very difficult' Ravi he explained unexpansively, thinking back to his own failed attempt. I nod not really able to comprehend what failing the selection had meant for him. 'But I heard, the selection criteria is much easier for British recruits to join the army' he asks with an almost hurt look on his face. 'It was', I replied.

Failing recruitment has long been a stressful, sad but inherent part of the Gurkha and the stringent acceptance criteria. In his book on the Gurkhas, Bryon Farwell writes that in the initial early stages of the Gurkha recruitment in the 19th-century failure to qualify had serious implications.

> *'Many of those who were rejected, for whatever reason, could not face returning to their homes with their disappointed hopes and dreams, so they stayed in India or perhaps found work in the Katmandu [sic] Valley.'*

The pressure riding on hopeful recruits was immense, entire households could benefit if they passed selection and could send wages home.

I, now slightly drunk, attempted to ask why he wanted to risk his life for a country that was not his own. *'Why'*, I ask, *'would you want to leave your home to fight you're a country that doesn't appreciate your efforts or give you equal pay'*. This was a system I felt was still firmly rooted in racial theories emanating from the 1800s

'Money', he replied deadpan, and I felt foolish. Moral scruples are a luxury and the price of inner reflection was higher than the salary's offered to Gurkhas. With few alternative opportunities available, serving as a Gurkha would bring more money, opportunities and pride for him and his family than waiting tables ever would.

As tough as the selection process and life as a Gurkhas was, many had a much better fate than many of their compatriots who ended up working as security guards in Iraq or Afghanistan, in June 2016 14 Nepalese security guards were killed guarding the Canadian Embassy in Kabul in June 2016, no Canadians were killed. This was far removed from the glamorous lives enjoyed by some other private military contractors, particularly western ones.

When I finished eating and stood up to leave Ravi shook my hand firmly and thanked me for talking. I still felt embarrassed by my questions. By trying to be inquisitive I had hinted at the almost feudal system of hired soldiers and if he saw it that way, as I know I did, my question had degraded, or at least cast some small dirt on the integrity of the Gurkhas. To take away a man's pride in his ancestors can be a horrible and morally capricious thing to do.

The next day waking early I nursed a hangover and said my goodbyes to Ravi, then after I checked out of the hotel and walked down to Tongba chowk, I got in a passing bus heading down to Dharan. The bus was predominately filled with older people; I was by far the youngest. Most I gathered from their collections of empty bags waiting to be filled at the bazaar were heading down to Dhankuta. Again it was not long before the talk on the bus, amongst the older men at least, turned inevitably to politics and the local election. We stopped at Dhankuta, most of the passengers got off. When after ten minutes the bus was full again, this time of mainly younger people, including one 20-year-old girl with an exam in Biratnagar that evening, we set off. As we rolled down the hills, the girl constantly flicked through the large stack of exam notes and past papers that she had brought with her.

Descending back down into Dharan, with local elections now only days away the police presence was large. The government had apparently recruited 75,000 temporary police officers to monitor and patrol the election. On every major chowk or junction, they stood, with lathis ready. Some, however, did not look a day over 18. If anything did kick off, this police looked as if they didn't have the training, strength or resolve to be effective. Moreover, despite being in the Terai, the majority of the police were paharias. A potential recipe for disaster, poorly trained, if at all, police from a dominant ethnic majority patrolling political tense areas of the Terai.

While there had been large amounts of political flags present on my way up Dharan, now returning only a few days later their number had somehow noticeably increased. Now Dharan was complete with Maoist bunting, hammer and sickles stretched out and draped themselves over street lights and electricity cables like the decorations on a particularly political Christmas tree. These competed with rival Congress and UML areas of town.

From Dharan, I got in a microbus to Biratnagar and Nepal's industrial heart belt. Heading south from Itarhi, we were flanked by large industries and factories. Yet most are, or look to the passing eye, abandoned and long closed down. Some particularly decrepit buildings had Maoist insignia daubed on the boundaries walls. It didn't take a long time to work out what happened. Union unrest. The overwhelming majority of the unions are politically affiliated, more often than not to the UML or Maoists, and often proved a useful staging post for aspiring politicians to make a name for themselves as an influential firebrand and as a result closures due to labour disputes were common. Many times it appeared the Maoists had indeed seized the methods of production, only to shut them down. Luckily Nepal's union problems were not quite as severe as India's, but still often posed a threat to Nepal's tired and under-resourced industrial sector, that was crying out for investment.

When we reached Biratnagar two hours after leaving Dharan, I got out of the bus, hailed a rickshaw and headed over to the bus park. I had spoken to my friends in Saptari but they were in Delhi, watching the cricket and tagging on a few meetings to make it a work trip, so I decided to head straight back to Kathmandu. At the bus park, I bought a ticket for the evening bus to Kathmandu. Having a few hours to kill I wandered over to a restaurant and ordered chicken khana. After eating I settled down to drink a beer, rest and to sweat in the almost now oppressive heat of the plains, it was almost 40 degrees. Biratnagar may have its charm, but it hides it well. Now, due to on-going road construction, the main road was surrounded by dust that whipped around you and reduced visibility to just a few metres. Two hours later, I boarded a night bus that would take me for the last time across half across the country that I have truly called home for the last three years.

The bus rolled down the dusty high street, pulled west at Ithari and we were back again on the East-West Highway. The sun was beginning to set, the road now was plied by an equal mix of buses, lorries and men and women on bicycles as I headed back to Kathmandu.

Epilogue

Pashupatinath

I parked my bike in a side street near Gaushala and walked past the rush-hour traffic down to the holy temple of Pashupatinath. Dedicated to Lord Shiva, evidence of Pashupatinath's existence dates back to 400 A.D and it is one of the most sacred temples in Hinduism. The main temple was constructed towards the end of the 17th century and is joined now by sprawling attached temples, lingams and forest stretching out behind it. I had come to watch the Bagmati Ganga Aarati. Considered the highest form of prayer, the aarati is a puja with priests chanting Vedic Mantras, playing a classical instrument and the lighting of Diyos, small oil lamps. It takes place daily along the banks of the holy Bagmati River, which murky waters will eventually find their way into the mighty Ganges, and it is conducted every night in Nepal and attracts hundreds of devotees on a daily basis.

I arrived considerably before the starting of the aarati and I wandered around the ruins and outskirts of the temple complex. It had rained heavily that day, the Bagmati swept past at speed, some funeral pyres along the burning Ghats spluttered and struggled to burn through the wet logs. The excess rain water poured down the stones and steps that lined Pashupatinath, the water streaming its way down to the river. The Bagmati river, after the rain, is dark, swollen and uncharacteristically rapid. I see a small lone blue chappal bounce along the river. The chapal bobbed along the dark river before vanishing from sight altogether along with its long and undulating journey to the Ganges and eventually the Bay of Bengal. One kid dove into the river from the ghats, another from the height of the bridge and another splashed aimlessly in the water. The kid who dived received much adulation from the younger crowd and shakes of despair and tuts of dissent from the more elderly congregation. At first, I watched in amazement, mainly at the bravery of jumping and swimming into such a dark swollen and undoubtedly disgusting dirty and polluted river. But maybe my amazement is wrong, it was May and previous trips this spring had shown the Bagmati to be a mere trickle, barely covering the river bank. Dogs, monkeys and street children bathed in its stagnant water. Now, however, the river was too high and fast for anyone to wash their clothes downstream of the ghats. Perhaps for these kids, it was their first swim since the flow of the Bagmati slowed last winter. I continued to watch the children jump into the swollen river.

It was a day after the first round of the first local elections for 20 years. The day before had been eerily quiet, with only a handful of bombs being diffused. Hundreds had been wounded in clashes, but vote rigging had mainly been prevented. The city had had a preoccupied feel as I wandered along the streets on election day. Today at the aarati, which had been held every day consistently for only 8 years but was first held in 200AD, there is a natural sense of continuity. These were new elections, but a sense of stability was preserved by an epoch old puja.

Now the arati began. After the initial invocation to Shiva, a Sanskrit prayer to the Bagmati River followed. I heard the flute, tabla and harmonium. But the music and prayers were only half of the spectacle. Three priests on the bank of the Bagmati lined up and each priest lifted fifty-four Diyos to Lord Shiva. They moved the Diyos around in a circle. The smell of incense was thick and the smoke danced in the light of the diyo.

I looked back at the crowd and thought over the last three years, studying in Nepal. Why so many people had asked incredulously. To Nepalese it was a slightly bemused question, so many times had I heard, *'but so many Nepalese goes to the UK to study, why did you come here?'* To Westerners, some could barely keep their distaste, or clear judgement of a poor decision out of their faces. *'Is the degree even worth anything'? 'Will anyone recognises it', 'Couldn't you have stayed in the UK'.* I had answered these questions to the best of my ability at first but soon grew tired. I felt now, staring into the flames of the diyo who had performed this same puja for so long it seemed like time immortal, that I was vindicated. If the point of further or graduate education was for education, I felt I couldn't have made a better choice. Standing here, the greatest asset I realised, had been the very thing that had dragged the most. The time, three years of study, interrupted by political instability, earthquakes and festivals, had allowed me to indulge myself to a dangerous level. Three years to read, to wander, to ask questions had been invaluable. Finding my studies often unsatisfactory had forced me to look elsewhere. A plethora of time led me to wander all over the valley, and then over Nepal. To wander the forgotten valleys.

The clouds darkened above us and they threatened to break, but for now, but they do not. The thunder echoed in the distance while the aarati continued. I saw three sadhus slouch off into the darkness towards the temples and ruins behind the main temple. It was dark now, too dark for the lucrative photos with tourists that keep many here, and is the main source of their income. They wouldn't be seen again until the next light, apart from perhaps if they are illuminated by the small glow of a candle with its light falling out of the many Shiva lingams they call home.

As the ringing of the bells and blowing on conch shells started to come to an end, signifying the end of the aarati, it was by now dark, the light from the lamps struggled to illuminate the ancient temple steps. It had started raining again. I walked back in the rain to my motorbike.

Glossary

Aarti	A religious ritual and form of devotion which involves the ceremonial use of lamps as part of a Puja
Bahulo	A colloquial term for someone suffering from mental illness
Brahmin/Bahun	The priest caste and the highest caste in the Varnas
Beedi	Cheap form of Indian cigarettes, tobacco wrapped in a tobacco leaf
Chapals	Sandals
Diyo	Small oil lamp
Doko	A wicker basket used to carry heavy loads, worn behind the head
Doti	A form of loin-cloth traditionally worn by North Indian males
Goonda	A hired thug, often in the pocket of politicians
Ghat	A series of stone steps leading down to a river, particularly sacred rivers.

Ghar	A house
Khana	A meal, most usually rice, dhal and vegetables
Ladoo	A popular milk based form of North Indian sweet, or Mithai
Lathi	A bamboo cane, often metal tipped, commonly used by police
Lingam	The phallic symbol commonly associated with Lord Shiva
Mahabharata	A Sanskrit epic
Mandir	Temple
Mukhtiyar	roughly equivalent to Prime Minister
Neta	a Political leader
Prasad	Offerings, typically food, left at a shrines
Puja	Religious devotions in the form of a small ceremony
Ramayana	A Sanskrit epic
Roti	Flat Indian Bread
Rook	Tree
Sadhu	A Hindu Holy man
Tal	A Lake

Bibliography

Baburam Acharaya. The Blood Stained Throne Struggles for Power in Nepal 1775-1914. Penguin Books. 2013

Byron Farwell. The Gurkhas: A history of the finest infantry men in the world. Penguin Books. 1985

Dr Harka Gurung. Vignettes of Nepal . Published by Sajha Prakashan. 1980

Dor Bahadur Bista. Fatalism and Development: Nepal's Struggle for modernization. Orient Black Swan. 2015

Francis Buchanan Hamilton. An Account of the Kingdom of Nepal and of the Territories Annexed to this Dominion by the House of Gorkha. Rupa Publications. 2007

Gabriele Tautscher. Himayan Mountain Cults-Sailung, Kalingchok and Gosainkund. Terriorial Rituals and Tamang Histories. Vajra Publications. 2007

Gustave Le Bon. Voyage to Nepal. This version published by Himal Books. 2014

Harka Gurung. Vignettes of Nepal. Sajha Prakashan. 1980

John Whelpton. A History of Nepal. Cambridge University Press. 2005

John Wheltpton, Micheal Hutt. The catalogue of the Hodgson Collection in the British Library. European Bulletin of Himalayan Research. Autumn-Winter. 2011

Kamal P. Malla the Road to Nowhere, A selection of Writings 1966-7. Published Jagadamba Prakashan. 2015

Kumar Pradhan. The Gorkha Conquests- The process and consequences of the unification of Nepal, with particular reference to Eastern Nepal. Published by Himal Books. 2006

Michel Peisell. Tiger for Breakfast, the story of Boris of Kathmandu- adventurer, big game hunter, and host of Nepal's famous Royal Hotel. Cambridge Press. Delhi. 1990

Ruedi Baumgartner. Farewell to Yak and Yeti? The Sherpas of Rolwaling facing a globalised world. Vajra Books. 2015

Patricia East, Susan Hoivik, Max Petrik, Sara Shneiderman and Mark Turin. The Gauri Shanker Trekking Area, A cultural tour book. Mandala Book Point. 2003

Prashant Jha. Battles of the New Republic: A contemporary History of Nepal. Aleph Book Company 2014